ANTI-INFLAMMATORY COOKBOOK

Affordable, Easy and Tasty Effective Recipes to Increase Your Sense of Liveliness and Energy. Soothe Your Immune System and Balance Your Body!

Includes a 60- DAY No-Stress Meal Plan

By
Lizzy McFields

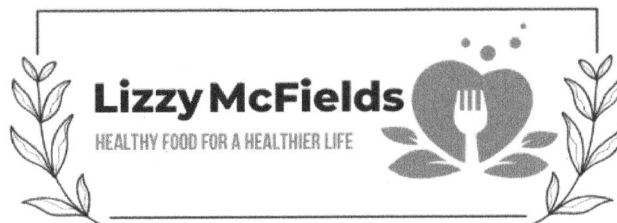

Lizzy McFields
HEALTHY FOOD FOR A HEALTHIER LIFE

Copyright© 2022 Lizzy McFields - All rights reserved. Edition 2023.

ISBN 979-8354689781
10 9 8 7 6 5 4 3 2 1

Book Editing and Proofreading by C.T.
Book Design, and front Cover Design by E.T. Design

Socials:
Facebook Page: @LizzyMcF
Facebook Private Group: Lizzy McFields Publishing
Instagram: lizzy_mcfields_publishing
Amazon Author Page: Lizzy Mcfields
Email: info@lizzymcf.com

All rights reserved.

Lizzy McFields
HEALTHY FOOD FOR A HEALTHIER LIFE

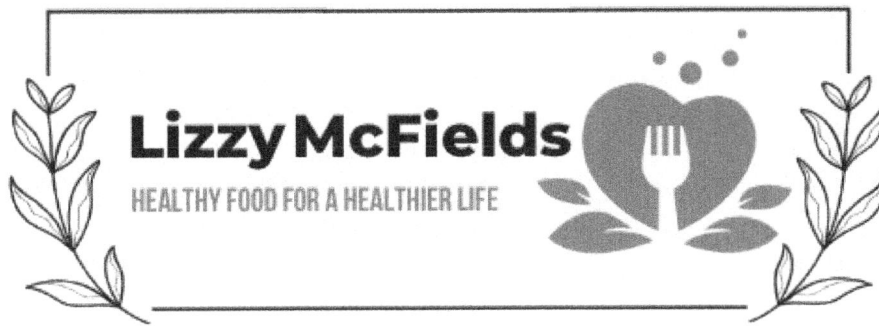

GET YOUR BONUS NOW!

Hello Fantastic Reader!

First, I would like to thank you for purchasing this Cookbook. I am sure it will be beneficial to improve your knowledge about this diet, especially your eating habits and overall well-being!

To prove my gratitude and appreciation for your trust in my scientific experience, I am happy to gift you with my food diary, "Daily Food Journal," which I am sure will make your health explode by tracking your daily progress. Don't wait any longer. Follow the instruction below to receive the digital copy for free! Enjoy your reading!

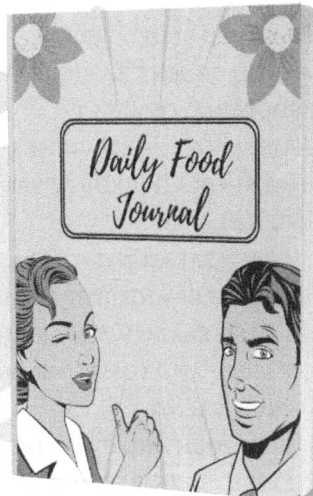

Daily Food Journal

Daily Food Sensitivity Journal

100 Day Food And Symptom Journal: Chronic Pain And Symptom Tracker.
Daily Food Log For Insomnia, Food Intolerance, Allergies, IBS Or Autoimmune Disease.

Become the Best Version of Yourself!

This bonus is **100% free**, with not string attached.
You don't need to enter any detail except your name and email address.

To download your bonus scan the QR code below

SCAN ME

Table of Contents

INTRODUCTION TO THE ANTI-INFLAMMATORY DIET

This book is intended as an easy to follow guide to understanding the anti-inflammatory diet. First of all, this is not just a diet, but a lifestyle. In fact, by consuming energetic and delicious whole foods in their natural state, you can achieve a body, cleansed of chronic inflammatory responses. This is about knowing the calories related to the nutrients and not counting calories. Here you will find only natural ingredients that benefit the human body.

Numerous scientific articles claim that eating healthily reduces chronic inflammation that may have settled in our bodies due to poor eating habits. Chronic inflammation is what chronic diseases, such as heart disease, diabetes, different types of arthritis, fibromyalgia, sciatica, hypertension, Alzheimer's disease, and cancer have in common. These diseases have the characteristic of inflaming organs, blood vessels, brain tissue, and joints.

The causes of chronic inflammation can be many. The leading "players" include stress, injured tissue, and eating foods that promote inflammation without having any anti-inflammatory ones in the diet. Nowadays, unfortunately, our food supply can contain many toxic compounds due to the widespread use of pesticides, genetically modified (GMO) crops, and runoff. Entirely toxin exposure is nearly impossible. However, you can limit your exposure and take some of the toxic burdens off your body by using organic foods.

Most of us have heard that belly fat is worse than hip and leg fat. Specifically, this accumulates around our abdominal organs. These abdominal fat cells, called adipocytes, are not static. They are metabolically active cells, especially when they are overfed. This can cause them to behave like a non-tissue and release many harmful hormones, such as tumor necrosis factor, IL-6, and free radicals. These hormones can cause tissue damage in other parts of the body, such as the inside of blood vessels. Therefore, the anti-inflammation diet should also include more efforts to reduce weight, especially belly fat! There are foods designed to stimulate this inflammatory reaction throughout the body. Others, however, tend to turn off the inflammation and help repair the damage.

I started a particular study on the anti-inflammatory diet to help my mother, who suffers from an autoimmune disease called fibromyalgia.

Fibromyalgia, a chronic disease of generalized pain, muscle weakness, sleep disturbances, chronic fatigue, and depression, affects many people worldwide.

Many of the symptoms of this disorder are said to be caused by antibodies that increase the activity of pain-sensitive nerves throughout the body. This condition leads to high levels of inflammation, which negatively affects health and can damage other body tissues and organs.

I have seen how this disease has affected my mother's quality of life. Unfortunately, we are not alone, as countless other people suffer from conditions associated with chronic inflammation and are tired of feeling sick or unable to do what they like (even simple things like playing a guitar). So, I decided to learn everything there is to know about inflammation and how to manage it.

Once I started my research, I became aware of the damage that chronic inflammation can cause, so I wanted to delve into how it can be prevented and reduced. Unfortunately, chronic inflammation can be a silent killer when left untreated because it can lead to severe illnesses as well. An Italian friend of mine always says, "we are what we eat," and there is no truer saying in this case.

And that's why I'm writing this book. I want to help anyone who wants to make the changes necessary to reduce their risk of developing inflammation-related diseases. This book is also for anyone who wants to learn how to eat mindfully and healthfully and give their body the best chance of staying healthy.

Proper nutrition is a significant investment in your health. When you eat poor-quality food, you are tapping into the nutrient reserves in your bones, soft tissues, organs, glands, skin, and even hair! We can all learn to eat better; we just need to get informed and, most importantly, want to!

Eating to reduce inflammation doesn't have to be a time-consuming ordeal. The principles in this book will help you select suitable foods and save time at the supermarket. You will choose foods that give you more energy than those that leave you exhausted. The recipes I provide in this book are quick and easy, so even your busiest day will allow you to eat healthily.

Let's start cooking together!

THE ANTI-INFLAMMATORY DIET EXPLAINED

UPSET BY INFLAMMATION?

Inflammation is a vital part of the body's defense mechanism and is very important for healing. However, sometimes things go haywire, and the processes supposed to help our bodies end up harming them. This is the case with chronic inflammation.

WHAT IS INFLAMMATION?

Inflammation is the immune system's response to an irritation in the body. This irritation could come from an injury, a disease, a foreign body, or a pathogen such as bacteria or a virus. The body, trying to protect itself, becomes inflamed. It happens by bringing in more blood to expel the foreign body or pathogen, thus beginning the healing process (Wawrzyniak-Gramacka et al., 2021).

There are five indicators of inflammation: a) redness due to increased blood flow, b) swelling, c) pain, d) heat and e) loss of function, which refers to reduced area mobility. But this is not always the case because sometimes inflammation does not present with any indicators and remains silent.

Inflammation is divided into two types: acute inflammation and chronic inflammation. Acute inflammation is a short-term event, for example, due to an injury. Chronic inflammation occurs long-term and can persist for months or, in extreme cases, years. This prolonged inflammation can cause the immune system to attack healthy organs and tissues, where the problem becomes more severe.

The inflammatory response develops in stages, involving various immune system cells that play specific roles. Here is a quick summary of what happens:

Invasion of healthy tissues by foreign substances (bacteria or viruses) causes infection.

Damaged or injured cells release substances that attract immune system cells. They send out actual chemical SOS signals that direct immune cells to the site of infection or injury.

Into the "combat zone" come macrophages or histiocytes that fight the invading germs. Through the bloodstream, other "soldiers" then arrive. The immune system's main fighters are white blood cells, also known as leukocytes. When the fight against foreign invaders intensifies, leukocytes release chemical molecules, including histamine, prostaglandins, and leukotrienes. These make the arteries dilate, allowing for more significant and faster blood flow and the arrival of more leukocyte reinforcements. This increased blood flow causes swelling, heat, redness, and discomfort typical of inflammation.

More generally, invading microbes are identified by dendritic cells. They evaluate the data and send signals to the immune cells best suited to kill that particular type of invading pathogen. For example, in a viral infection, they call on CD-8 T lymphocytes because they are cells that specialize in eliminating viruses. When the invading germs are of a different type, other types of immune cells are summoned. The "enemy" information is also passed on to so-called memory cells (T-killer lymphocytes) to activate immediately in case the same (or similar) pathogen tries to attack our body again. It is through this process that long-term immunity is created.

The main mechanisms of killing these pathogens are phagocytosis (cells engulf the pathogen) and cytotoxicity (release of chemicals that can kill it).

Once the "battle" is over, the leukocytes return to the bloodstream.

Phagocytosis is a process that removes or cleans up dead cells. Most of this cleaning is done by macrophages, which eat the waste and dead cells.

Fibroblasts are "engineer" cells that heal the damage and rebuild the inflammatory site. After a while, the area returns to its pre-inflammation state.

Because many immune cells are involved, this process can seem confusing. Each cell has a distinct role, and they all work together in a structured and systematic way. The entire defense process can be completed in minutes or even hours in some cases. Acute inflammation is temporary and lasts only a few days.

The inflammation process can be simplified by thinking of it as having two phases: pro-inflammatory and anti-inflammatory.

Several immune cells fight the disease in the initial phase by removing or neutralizing invading bacteria. These immune cells arrive in waves, each continuing the work of the previous wave. During this time, "preparatory cells" and "fighting cells" are the most active at this point that the usual inflammatory symptoms appear.

The pro-inflammatory process is reversed in the second (anti-inflammatory) phase. When the immune cells have completed their task, they retreat. Repair and rebuilding will continue until the body is restored to its previous state of normalcy. The "cleansing" and "repair" cells are now the most active cells.

The immune cells that make up most inflammatory processes are composed of essential fatty acids. Our bodies do not naturally produce these, so we must supplement them with food. The fats that our body needs are: Omega-3 and omega-6.

Omega-3 fatty acids are involved in the anti-inflammatory phase, and are primarily concerned with repair and cleansing. Omega-6 fatty acids play a role against invading microbes (pro-inflammatory phase). Omega-3s, on the other hand, tend to reduce or even prevent inflammation, while omega-6s increase or even cause inflammation.

This information is essential because it allows us to understand which foods can help reduce inflammation and thus treat the symptoms of inflammatory diseases such as rheumatoid arthritis.

ACUTE INFLAMMATION

The inflammation disappears quickly in most cases once the problem is resolved. It usually lasts a few minutes or hours, although it can last up to a few days.

The inflammation goes away once the injury is recovered and healed.

Allergies also cause an acute inflammatory reaction. When you eat something you are allergic to or are allergic to something in the air, these foreign substances are attacked by your immune system. You may experience typical signs of inflammation such as itching, rashes, swollen joints, and colds. These symptoms usually subside once the allergen is eliminated.

The infection or injury may not be limited to a single body part. It could also be systemic, affecting the entire body, such as viral diseases like influenza. The initial immune system response is the same: inflammation.

The only difference is that symptoms may take longer to appear and fade. For example, the person may first feel only fatigue, followed by a burning sensation in the eyes or joints, possibly chills, and finally fever.

These symptoms indicate that the immune system is working hard to rid the body of the disease. These indications will eventually go away on their own. On the other hand, anti-inflammatory medications can relieve symptoms more quickly, but only under medical consultation.

Although the signs of acute inflammation may be painful or unpleasant, they are evidence of a robust and functioning immune system.

HOW DO I KNOW IF I AM EXPERIENCING INFLAMMATION?

Many factors can increase the risk of inflammatory responses in your body. These factors include:

Diet: Saturated or trans fats - found in dairy products, red meat, baked goods, and fried foods - are associated with higher inflammation-causing molecules in the body. The same goes for refined sugar and highly processed foods.

Obesity: Studies have shown a connection between high adipose tissue levels and the production of molecules that cause inflammation (Kendel et al., 2020). These studies have found that fat levels and inflammation-causing molecules increase proportionally.

Stress and Sleep Disorders: This is important to consider because stress is a big problem for many people worldwide. Modern life has become extremely fast-paced and can be very challenging to our health. Emotional and physical stress can cause an increase in the production of molecules that cause inflammation. Irregular sleep patterns can have the same effect.

Age: As we age, we produce more inflammation-causing molecules in our bodies.

Smoking: Smoking cigarettes decreases inflammation-fighting molecules needed to keep inflammation levels in a healthy range.

Rheumatoid Arthritis: Those genetically predisposed to this condition may develop rheumatoid arthritis due to an autoimmune response to external irritants such as smoking. This autoimmune response causes inflammation of the joints that, over time, can lead to further complications.

Chronic kidney disease: Inflammation is a standard part of this disease. It can lead to inflammation-causing molecules in the blood that further aggravate the condition and cause death.

Low levels of sex hormones: Hormones such as estrogen and testosterone have been found to inhibit the production of inflammation-causing molecules in our bodies. The suppressive effect cannot occur if the levels of these hormones are low.

Chronic inflammation can also develop from sensitivity or long-term exposure to an irritant, for example, a chemical in the air.

Pulmonary Diseases: Chronic Obstructive Pulmonary Disease (COPD) is a lung disease that presents as a chronic inflammatory response to irritants in the lungs and can lead to long-term problems with breathing.

Cardiovascular disease: Chronic inflammation can lead to atherosclerosis, which is present when a fatty plaque full of cholesterol builds up inside your arteries. Your body can then mistake this plaque for a foreign substance and may respond with inflammation to stop the damage. This inflammation can lead to other serious cardiovascular problems such as a stroke.

Inflammatory Bowel Disease: This is a group of diseases associated with chronic inflammation of the digestive tract. It can start as ulcerative colitis that causes long-term inflammation and ulcers in the rectum or large intestine. Crohn's disease represents an example of inflammatory bowel disease.

Common symptoms of chronic inflammation include:
- recurrent infections
- mood swings, depression, and anxiety
- pain in the body
- acid reflux, diarrhea, or constipation
- insomnia and chronic fatigue

The diagnosis of chronic inflammation can be made with the help of a blood test. Unfortunately, these levels are usually only checked when another medical condition is causing the inflammation. Because of this, many people suffer from chronic inflammation without ever being diagnosed.

As previously said, inflammation is one of the most common factors that causes or contributes to the development of chronic diseases. Fortunately, you can reduce your risk of inflammation by making smarter, healthier food choices. The foods we eat can significantly act on inflammatory effects. By choosing your food wisely - which means selecting anti-inflammatory foods and avoiding foods that promote inflammation - you can prevent inflammation and all the dangers that come with it. Feeding your body with anti-inflammatory foods gives your immune system the resources to function well and keep chronic disease at bay.

By learning which foods prevent inflammation, you can focus more on eating the nutrients to support your health and healing. Your body won't have to spend as much energy defending itself. Following an anti-inflammatory diet can be simple. If you find that you have been eating foods that cause inflammation, don't worry. After you learn which foods promote inflammation and which ones help prevent it, you can start making gradual changes to your diet. Keep adding anti-inflammatory foods and eliminating inflammatory foods until you have completely transitioned to an anti-inflammatory diet.

References:
Wawrzyniak-Gramacka E, Hertmanowska N, Tylutka A, Morawin B, Wacka E, Gutowicz M, Zembron-Lacny A. The Association of Anti-Inflammatory Diet Ingredients and Lifestyle Exercise with Inflammaging. Nutrients. 2021 Oct 21;13(11):3696. doi: 10.3390/nu13113696.

Ken el Jovanovi G, Mrakovcic-Sutic I, Pavi i e elj S, Šuša B, Raheli D, Klobu ar Majanovi S. The Efficacy of an Energy-Restricted Anti-Inflammatory Diet for the Management of Obesity in Younger Adults. Nutrients. 2020 Nov 22;12(11):3583. doi: 10.3390/nu12113583.

ANTI-INFLAMMATORY DIET: HEALTH BENEFITS

There are numerous health benefits to following an anti-inflammatory diet. Surprisingly, it offers similar benefits to the most popular diet (the Mediterranean diet). We'll go through all the main benefits of this diet. Remember that there is a personal component. This means that some foods that do not cause inflammation may, in some people, still lead to inflammatory sensations. We must know how to recognize these signs, interpret them, and avoid (even among the anti-inflammatory foods) what causes discomfort.

DETOXIFYING YOUR BODY, CLEANSING YOUR CELLS AND BOOST YOUR IMMUNE SYSTEM

Detoxifying the body is especially crucial to living a long and healthy life; however, many people detoxify their bodies using juice cleanses or other procedures that do not work. The anti-inflammatory diet has been proven to help detoxify the body at the cellular and gut level, and is much more superior to a body cleanse.

As you may know, an anti-inflammatory diet detoxifies your body at the cellular level through autophagy; this process eats up bad cells and replaces them with healthier and much stronger cells. Through this procedure, you'll notice benefits like a stronger immune system, disease prevention, insulin sensitivity, and a lower risk of developing cancer. Overall, the anti-inflammatory diet detoxifies your body on a cellular level. Let's look at how the anti-inflammatory diet might help you detoxify on a digestive level.

The anti-inflammatory diet has been shown to help cleanse the gut. We need to give our digestive system a break from regularly eating all those bad or junk foods.

Your body will focus on digesting the meal rather than cleaning up the toxins. It will start to clean out your stomach, which is beneficial for those who have a lot of cleaning up to do, but it will also help you digest your food and think more clearly. Cleansing your body helps reduce your disease risk, allowing you to live a longer and healthier life.

There's a reason why having a good immune system is so important: it helps you avoid getting sick and you become more "immune" to disease. Since the anti-inflammatory diet has been shown to boost the immune system, we'll talk about how it does it. A stem cell study was conducted in the context of a human diet to determine how stem cells renew themselves.

As you may know, the anti-inflammatory diet has been shown to lower insulin levels, which is excellent news for anyone looking to boost their immune system. One study found that high insulin levels make it difficult for "T" cells to function correctly. "T" cells fight disease and inflammation by suppressing inflammation. "T" cells are primarily responsible for removing toxins that cause infection and inflammation. When insulin levels are high, "T" cells do not function to their full potential, causing our immune system to deteriorate.

There is no need for insulin spikes when dieting, which allows our bodies to help the "T" cells function better, improving our immune system overall. If you don't eat meals that make your insulin spike, your digestive system and organs will get a break. When you eat a large meal, your stomach gets about 70% of the blood and energy to digest it. This means that you allow your body to recover when you are on a diet. Everything heals when you follow an anti-inflammatory diet, including your digestive system. Once you give your gut some time to recover, it will be much more effective.

REDUCE STRESS AND INFLAMMATION

As we have already mentioned, inflammation is known to cause various chronic diseases, including Alzheimer's, dementia, obesity, diabetes, and many others. The anti-inflammatory diet can now help you get rid of inflammation in several ways. The first is autophagy; as you may know, an anti-inflammatory diet aids in cell renewal by eliminating dead ones. If your body doesn't renew cells, old ones that have been around for a long time can create inflammation because they are full of metabolic waste products.

Now that we've discussed a variety of options of how an anti-inflammatory diet helps you reduce inflammation; let's look at how an anti-inflammatory diet can help you overcome stress. Inflammation and stress go hand in hand. If you are stressed, maybe you feel that your body is experiencing inflammation. This means that lowering inflammation will reduce your stress levels, and as you may know, this diet promotes better brain function. An anti-inflammatory diet allows you to send better messages to your brain, resulting in a more efficient brain.

When your mind is working at its full potential, your stress levels are lowered; increased brain function can also help you get rid of any stress you're experiencing and improve your overall health, which can help you lose weight. Overall, the health benefits of the anti-inflammatory diet will help you eliminate or at least reduce stress.

PREVENTING DISEASE

In today's world, there are numerous diseases. This implies that we need to find a technique to lower the risk of diseases to improve overall health and wellness. It has already been shown the anti-inflammatory has the ability to reduce the risk of several major diseases. Alzheimer's and Parkinson's disease are two examples of the many ailments that an anti-inflammatory diet can help with.

As you may know, an anti-inflammatory diet helps improve brain health and reduce the risk of neurological diseases. An anti-inflammatory diet has been shown in some studies to help reduce the risk of depression. At the same time, some people may not consider depression a disorder, but it is still a serious problem in our society.

Anti-inflammatory diets have also been shown to lower cholesterol levels and also help those with type 2 diabetes by reducing, if not eliminating, insulin intake in some cases. While we don't recommend it if you have type 2 diabetes, it does demonstrate the importance of nutrition and insulin resistance.

Despite this, numerous studies suggest that an anti-inflammatory diet can reduce the risk of diabetes and should be used preventatively.

Cancer is another debilitating condition that can be helped by following an anti-inflammatory diet. As you may know, the anti-inflammatory diet allows you to create a less friendly environment for cancer cells, making it a good choice for those looking to lower their risk.

WEIGHT LOSS

As you may know, there are numerous methods for losing weight. Having said that,, the anti-inflammatory diet is one of the most popular weight loss methods, and for a good reason. Many individuals do not know that the anti-inflammatory diet is one of the most effective ways to lose "body fat" rather than "bodyweight." Most diets cause people to lose a lot of weight, but it is usually a loss of muscle and water weight.

On the other hand, the anti-inflammatory diet makes you lose more body fat. Here's how it works: your glycogen stores are depleted as your caloric intake decreases when you eat the right healthy foods over a long period. This causes the body to draw on its stores, which are of course, your body fat. This is good for people who want to reduce weight because you burn more body fat than muscle mass or glycogen. Also, as you may know, a healthy diet has a significant impact on your hormones. Your insulin levels will stabilize, while your growth hormone levels will increase, allowing your body to burn body fat healthily.

INCREASED LONGEVITY

Many studies have shown that an anti-inflammatory diet can improve longevity. As we mentioned earlier, an anti-inflammatory diet can help with cellular regeneration. This diet has been shown to promote longevity and overall well-being.

IS THE ANTI-INFLAMMATORY DIET A LIFESTYLE?

HOW TO GET RID OF INFLAMMATION

To lower your risk of chronic inflammation, you have to make positive changes to your diet and lifestyle. When you constantly eat inflammatory foods, they will negatively affect your body. Likewise, chronic inflammation will stay in your body if you continue to use unhealthy habits. The anti-inflammatory diet is just one aspect of leading a healthier life. Before we get into the specifics of the anti-inflammatory diet, let's discuss the most practical and effective tips for reducing inflammation.

REGULAR EXERCISE

Regular exercise is essential if you want to reduce or prevent inflammation. For best results, try to exercise every single day. Vary your exercise routine and try to have fun! If you don't feel motivated to exercise alone, you can try joining a class online or at a gym, where you can work out with other people. Suppose exercise isn't part of your current lifestyle, then in that case, you can start gradually by adding more physical activities to your day, such as walking to work, taking the stairs instead of the elevator, or even walking around the office for every 30 minutes you spend at your desk.

LEARN HOW TO MANAGE STRESS

I've mentioned before that stress can cause or contribute to chronic inflammation. You want to avoid high levels of stress, and you can do that by learning how to manage stress more effectively. There are many ways to do this, such as learning time management, meditation, biofeedback, or yoga. Which one works best for you?

REACHING A HEALTHY WEIGHT

People who are obese or overweight are more prone to inflammation. If you know you fall into these categories, by following the recommendations specified in this book and sticking to this diet, you could start shedding those stubborn excess pounds. Since this diet is healthy and balanced, your body will be happy to eliminate the unnecessary deposits, usually in excess fat and water. When you start losing weight, you will also be able to decrease inflammation in your body and its risks.

CONSIDER FASTING

Have you ever considered following the eating pattern of intermittent fasting (IF)? Fasting can be very beneficial in terms of reducing inflammation. And the beauty of IF is that there are several ways to do it. Combining intermittent fasting with an anti-inflammatory diet can lead to wonderful results. Try it by starting with spontaneous skipping of meals and progressing to longer fasting windows. Your body will thank you.

DON'T ALLOW YOURSELF TO BE "HUNGRY"

When it comes to fasting, you should do it gradually. Otherwise, you may end up feeling "hungry." When you feel so hungry, you get angry about every little thing. Although 'hangry' is not a technical term, it describes the situation perfectly. When you're hungry, you tend to overeat. What's worse, you'll crave unhealthy foods that are typically inflammatory.

TAKE A BREAK FROM ALCOHOL

Because excessive alcohol consumption can cause inflammation, you may want to take a (temporary) break from alcohol. If you're the type of person who likes to have a glass of wine, a bottle of beer, or a cocktail every night, consider curbing the craving for a couple of days. Doing this will help your body calm down, reducing any inflammation within your body. Then, you can get back into your routine, but this time, opt for healthier alcoholic beverages that don't contain added sugar.

Of course, if you want to reduce inflammation and improve your long-term health, you may want to give up alcohol consumption altogether. I understand that this is one of the hardest things to do, especially since enjoying a glass of red wine after a long, tiring day sounds pretty relaxing, but your body will appreciate it! If you're still unsure, why not experiment with a "7 Day Challenge" where you give up alcohol and replace it with a healthier habit, like going to bed early. Do this for at least seven days and see how your health improves. Then, try maintaining this habit for a longer period of time…

Get enough sleep every night

These days, we feel like we don't have enough time during the day to do everything we want or need to do. Because of this, we tend to stay up late to finish all our tasks on time. In some cases, people stay up because it's the only time they can relax and unwind. But isn't it much more relaxing to fall asleep early? It's also healthier. Getting enough sleep each night (seven to eight hours) helps your body rest and repair itself. But if you routinely get less than the recommended hours of sleep, this can exacerbate inflammation in your body and lead to chronic inflammation.

Picky Eating

While being a picky eater is not a good thing for kids, as an adult, this is something you need to start practising. Whether you're choosing ingredients for cooking or looking for ready-to-eat foods, it's important to check labels to make sure you're only getting healthy products.

Choose anti-inflammatory foods

Finally, you should start following an anti-inflammatory diet. This is a very easy diet because it is not too strict or restrictive. You simply have to learn to make healthier choices in terms of food and follow a couple of simple guidelines to make you healthier. For example, you will need to load up on fruits and vegetables, flavor your meals with herbs and spices, introduce probiotics into your diet, minimize dairy consumption, and make other adjustments to "clean up" your current diet.

You are now ready to learn more about the anti-inflammatory diet with these tips in mind. This is probably the most significant of all the lifestyle changes you need to make, so read on!

FIVE HOBBIES FOR A HEALTHY LIFESTYLE

To live better as we age, we still need to stay healthy inside and out. We have the opportunity to do the same things we did when we were younger or try something different. Introduce into your daily routine not only a healthy diet but also exercise. If you're not sure where to start, here are some hobby suggestions to help you live a healthier lifestyle:

GARDENING

Gardening isn't just a pastime for retirees or those with lots of free time. It's a great way to relieve tension and keep your body active. Gardening is not only excellent for the body, it's also calming. Learn how to garden properly by joining a club or starting independently. Gardening is an excellent opportunity to meet new people and a great way to get away from the hectic world we live in today. You'll be away from the traffic, pollution, and noise even if you're in a city!

DRAW

Drawing is an excellent activity where children and adults an be taught to draw creatively. Simply get a piece of paper and a pencil and get started. You can learn and understand how to make real art step by step. It's not easy at first, but if you stay focused, you will succeed. Lines, triangles, circles, and various other shapes can be learned. Make a drawing of a friend or your child's face, or look at any of the beautiful artwork you are surrounded by.

PAINTING

Anyone can paint, and it is a great joy to do so. Just grab a paintbrush and paint a splash of color on a canvas or wall. To enjoy splashing color all over the place, you don't need to be an artist. You'll learn to appreciate the work of others and get inspiration of your own. It's also a fantastic opportunity to get away from the computer and TV and focus on your projects.

CREATIVE WRITING

Creative writing can be a beautiful way to express yourself, learn to put your ideas and thoughts into words, and communicate with others. All you need is an idea to write about, a topic and start writing.

Start somewhere if you don't want to get stuck with writer's block. You could start with a blank sheet on your computer, an idea from your life, or a movie. You'll be surprised how much you can write in a short period.

SINGING

Singing isn't just for women. Men can learn to sing as well. Many individuals don't like their voice, but you'll be surprised at how horrible you once sounded if you don't like the way you sing now. Singing helps develop vocal control and the ability to hit various pitches. To enjoy singing, you don't have to be a great singer.

ANTI-INFLAMMATORY DIET PRINCIPLES

The anti-inflammatory diet doesn't just reduce or prevent inflammation; the very nature of this diet promotes long-term health. By lowering inflammation in your body, you can also lower your risk of developing other diseases. It also helps increase your metabolism and slow down the aging process. Although this diet doesn't have strict rules, it has some important principles. Here are the basic principles of this diet:

Consume plenty of foods rich in omega-3 fatty acids, such as oily fish. Eating oily fish is important. You should do it at least three times a week.

Eat plenty of fruits, vegetables, and whole grains. These contain fiber, minerals, vitamins, and antioxidants that calm the body and help prevent inflammation.

Opt for oils that contain healthy fats for cooking or adding flavor to your dishes.

Enhance your dishes using natural ingredients such as herbs, spices, and natural sweeteners when cooking.

As long as they are anti-inflammatory, snacks are fine.

Reduce your consumption of dairy products except for kefir, yogurt, or anything fermented.

Minimize your sugar intake (especially refined sugar) and refined carbohydrates such as white rice or white bread.

Eliminate trans fats from your diet. This means you should stay away from all foods that contain trans fats in their list of ingredients.

Avoid processed foods as much as possible. They contain ingredients that cause inflammation. Over time, try eliminating them from your diet altogether and replacing them with whole, natural foods.

As you can see, the anti-inflammatory diet principles are very simple. Even if you plan to switch to a different type of diet in the future, these principles will give you a great advantage. If you choose to keep this diet as the basis of your eating habits, you can be sure that your health will improve over time. Your body will begin to learn how to use inflammation efficiently and only when it is needed.

BASIC DIET GUIDELINES

Another great thing about this diet is that you can follow it easily, as long as you are familiar with its principles: the basic diet guidelines are based on these principles. To help you understand them, let's briefly discuss each of these guidelines.

Eat more vegetables and fruits

Fruits, vegetables, herbs, and spices should be your main focus in this diet. These contain numerous vitamins, minerals, essential nutrients, antioxidants, and phytonutrients - and all of these offer anti-inflammatory benefits. Following this diet doesn't mean you have to give up meat, but it would be better for you, in the long run, to learn to eat more plant-origin foods, preferably at every meal.

For centuries, plants have been used to treat various diseases, many associated with inflammation. These plant-based remedies and medications have been so effective that they are still used today. With this in mind, imagine how healthy you will be if you make these plants part of your regular diet. You can eat vegetables and fruits raw, add them to your dishes or even eat them as snacks. No matter how you add the plants to your diet, these nutritious foods will help you reduce or prevent inflammation in your body.

EAT ANCIENT AND WHOLE GRAINS

Ancient grains have undergone minimal changes through selective breeding compared to other grains such as rice, corn, and some wheat varieties that have changed significantly. For this reason, ancient grains are believed to be healthier than modern varieties. Some examples of ancient grains are spelt, sorghum, oats, barley, chia, amaranth, and buckwheat.

Whole grains contain bran, germ, and endosperm, unlike refined grains that contain only the endosperm. These grains are also considered healthier because they also contain more fiber. Whole grain examples are brown rice, barley, and rye (although the latter two should be avoided if you have celiac disease or gluten intolerance). Adding these grains to your diet is essential because they are rich in nutrients, antioxidants, and other anti-inflammatory substances.

Eat healthy fats

Healthy fats sources are nuts, olive oil, avocados, salmon, and other fatty fish, which contain omega-3 and omega-6 components known to be anti-inflammatory. Because the body can't produce these essential fatty acids on its own, you need to get them from your diet. Fortunately, there are many delicious ways to add healthy fats to your diet and reduce inflammation in your body.

EAT NUTS AND SEEDS

In addition to chia seeds and walnuts, which contain healthy fats, other types of nuts and seeds are part of this diet. These contain monounsaturated and polyunsaturated fats, which can help lower cholesterol levels. They also contain omega-3s, which, as you know, offer anti-inflammatory benefits. Some nuts also contain vitamin E and l-arginine, which can help keep inflammation in check. Just try to avoid overdoing it, especially when eating them as a snack.

For example, since the recommended daily value of walnuts is between 30 and 60 grams, you should only eat 5 to 10 walnuts. It is good to measure an appropriate portion of nuts in a small bowl or plate. Avoid snacking directly from a bag or bottle of nuts. Also, remember that some types of nuts can cause inflammation due to an allergic reaction. Nut varieties such as almonds, pecans, cashews, and hazelnuts, for example, can cause allergic reactions in some people, so you should do some trial and error first to determine the effect of different varieties.

ADD FLAVOR WITH HERBS AND SPICES

Rather than adding too much sugar or salt to your dishes, opt for herbs and spices to make your food more flavorful. These plants typically contain a wide range of beneficial nutrients, many of which are anti-inflammatory. Some of the best herbs and spices are ginger, turmeric, and garlic. These are considered powerful anti-inflammatories, and adding them to your meals will make your culinary masterpieces more flavorful.

SUPPORT YOUR MICROBIOME

To do this, you need to eat foods that contain probiotics. These are considered "good bacteria" and help lower the levels of inflammation in your body. Supporting your microbiome is even more important when you suffer from inflammatory diseases because probiotics can help improve the effects of treatment.

Eat fewer processed foods

Processed foods are commonly associated with obesity and many chronic diseases. They are considered high glycemic index foods that stimulate inflammation in the body. To follow the anti-inflammatory diet, you need to disabuse yourself of these foods gradually. Remember that this diet is clean and natural. By eliminating processed foods, you can help reduce inflammation in your body and the amount of free radical damage these foods contain.

CONSUME LESS MEAT

Although lean meat is fine in moderation, you should try to limit your consumption of red meat and processed meat products. These contain saturated fats, which are known to cause inflammation as well. If you are a meat lover, try to learn how to prepare dishes that will help you overcome your meat cravings without restricting yourself completely. Once in a while, you can consume red meat, especially while transitioning to the anti-inflammatory diet.

RELAX

High-stress levels or prolonged stress can cause an overproduction of cortisol. When this happens, your body's ability to regulate its immune and inflammatory responses loses effectiveness. Aside from your diet, you may want to learn how to manage your stress more effectively. Combine this with a healthier, cleaner diet, and you're sure to start feeling

better.

After trying this diet to eliminate inflammation, you can switch to a healthy maintenance eating style like the Mediterranean Diet (upcoming book).

WHAT CAN I EAT?

Food Group	Recommended Foods
Vegetables	Acorn squash, Arugula, Beets, Brussels sprouts, Cabbage, Carrots, Cassava, Cauliflower, Celery leaves, Collards, Fennel, Kale, Leeks, Lettuce, Mustard greens, Okra, Parsnip, Rutabaga, Scallions, Sea vegetables, Spaghetti squash, Spinach, Sweet potato, Turnips, Watercress, Winter squash
Legumes, Nuts, and seeds	Almonds, Flax, Hazelnuts*, Kidney beans, Navy beans, Pistachios, Soybeans, Sunflower seeds*, Walnuts*
Protein	Free-range eggs*, Anchovies, Herring, Mackerel, Oysters, Salmon, Sardines, Trout, Tuna, Poultry (pasture-raised, wild, grass-fed meats)
Healthy Fats	Avocado oil, Coconut oil, Grapeseed oil, Olive oil
Fruit	Apples, Apricots, Bananas, Oranges, Pineapple, Strawberries
Carbohydrates	Barley, Brown rice, Bulgur, Oatmeal, Quinoa, Whole-wheat flour*
Herbs and Spices	Cinnamon, Cloves, Ginger, Rosemary, Sage Thyme, Oregano
Probiotics	Coconut milk kefir, Coconut milk yogurt, Fermented fruit, Fermented vegetables, Kombucha, Water kefir
Others	Cocoa and dark chocolate, coffee, green tea
Organ Meat	Connective tissues, skin, joints, and bone broth (contain nutrients that may help reduce inflammation.)

*Foods That are Both Inflammatory and Anti-Inflammatory

WHAT TO LIMIT?

However, there are several foods you should avoid when eating Anti-Inflammatory meals.

ALCOHOLIC DRINKS (IN EXCESS)

Moderate alcohol consumption is not harmful; it can even be beneficial. But drinking in excess can cause many problems, one of which is inflammation. The main problem is that excess alcohol can cause issues with bacterial toxins leaving the colon and entering the body. This condition, known as "leaky gut," causes inflammation. To avoid this, limit your alcohol consumption to healthy levels.

ARTIFICIAL TRANS FATS

This type of fat is probably the unhealthiest fat out there.

If you read food ingredient lists, you may see this ingredient as "partially hydrogenated oils." Artificial trans fats are typically added to processed foods to extend their shelf life. Unfortunately, the consumption of this ingredient increases the risk of inflammation. Some examples of foods that may contain artificial trans fats are:

- Any processed food product that contains partially hydrogenated oil
- Packaged cookies
- Fried fast food
- Margarine (some varieties)
- Vegetable shortening
- Packaged cakes
- French fries
- Packaged pastries
- Microwave popcorn (some varieties)

DAIRY PRODUCTS

In general, dairy products such as milk and cheese contain high amounts of saturated fat, increasing the risk of inflammation. This is especially true for whole-grain dairy products. In some cases, severe or chronic inflammation can also cause lactose intolerance.

OVERNIGHT PRODUCTS.

Although nightshade roots are very nutritious, they can potentially cause inflammation. The main reason for this is the solanine content. This chemical can exacerbate inflammation in the body. Some examples of nightshades are:

- Paprika
- Eggplant
- Goji berries
- Cayenne
- Tomatillos
- Potatoes (except sweet potatoes)

REFINED CARBOHYDRATES

When refined carbohydrates are processed, most of the fiber they contain is removed. These carbohydrates tend to increase inflammation in the body and blood sugar levels. Some examples of foods with refined carbohydrates are:

- All types of processed foods that contain added flour or sugar
- Cookies
- Pies
- Pasta
- Bread
- Soft drinks

- Candy
- Cereals (some varieties)
- Confectionery

SOME TYPES OF CEREALS

In general, grains do not cause inflammation. But wheat, barley, and rye are grains that contain gluten, which can lead to inflammation in people with celiac disease, wheat allergy, or non-celiac gluten sensitivity. You should avoid these grains if you suffer from one of these conditions. Otherwise, you don't have to eliminate them from your diet.

SUGAR

High-fructose corn syrup and table sugar don't belong in your diet because they also increase inflammation. Unfortunately, many food products contain these ingredients, so you need to be extra careful when buying sweets. Some examples of foods that contain added sugar are:

- Chocolate
- Donuts
- Cereals (some varieties)
- Candy
- Sweet pastries
- Cakes
- Soft drinks
- Cookies

RED AND PROCESSED MEAT

Although lean meat is fine in moderation, red meat and processed meat products are huge no-nos. These foods increase the risk of inflammation and a host of chronic diseases. Processed meats also contain high amounts of advanced glycation end products, known to increase inflammation. Some examples of processed and red meats are:

- Beef jerky
- Canned meat
- Hamburgers
- Bacon
- Smoked meat
- Salami
- Sausages
- Steaks
- Hot dogs
- Ham

VEGETABLE OILS

Vegetables are part of your diet, but oils derived from vegetables are another story. Because most vegetable oils are highly processed, they usually contain excessive amounts of omega-6. Unhealthy amounts of this fatty acid can cause inflammation, especially if you suffer from inflammatory conditions such as irritable bowel syndrome or arthritis.

OTHER INFLAMMATORY FOODS

Other foods that don't fall into the previous categories but can still cause inflammation. These include:

- Ready-to-eat meals
- Artificial sweeteners
- Foods high in sodium, such as chips and other junk foods
- Energy drinks
- Egg rolls
- Fried chicken
- Sports drinks
- Sweet tea
- Mozzarella sticks
- Pretzels

Many of these foods appear in more than one category. This indicates that such foods are truly inflammatory, and you should stay away from them as much as possible.

FOODS THAT ARE BOTH INFLAMMATORY AND ANTI-INFLAMMATORY

As you familiarize yourself with these food lists and start planning your meals, you should know that some foods can have inflammatory and anti-inflammatory effects. You may have noticed some foods on the anti-inflammatory list that have asterisks - these are the foods to watch out for.

FREE-RANGE EGGS

Free-range eggs are incredibly healthy, but they affect people in various ways. Factors such as existing illnesses and a person's weight can impact whether or not free-range eggs cause inflammation in the body. This is especially true for egg whites. For this reason, you should observe your body immediately after eating free-range eggs to check if you experience any adverse effects, which may indicate inflammation.

If you find that free-range eggs don't agree with you, you can use egg substitutes in recipes that call for this ingredient. You can use commercial egg substitutes, such as vegan liquid yolks, and make your egg substitutes in your kitchen. You can use tofu, chickpea brine, or even fruits like bananas or pumpkin if you prefer homemade options. Look in health food stores for these healthy substitutes, so you can continue to create delicious recipes even though they contain free-range eggs.

LEGUMES, NUTS, AND SEEDS

Probably the riskiest legume you can eat in terms of inflammation is peanuts. Although peanuts are very common, they contain a family of toxins known as aflatoxins, which can potentially stimulate an inflammatory response in your body. For other legumes, the inflammatory effect may stem from their lectin content. Because lectins are difficult for the body to break down, this can cause inflammation. In addition to legumes, other examples of nuts and seeds that can cause inflammation include:

- Nut butter
- Seed-based spices
- Nut oils
- Walnut flours
- Seed oils

NIGHTSHADE PRODUCTS

One of the most commonly avoided types of vegetables is nightshades when it comes to inflammation. It's important to know that many of the foods we consume contain minute amounts of solanine, the compound that triggers inflammation. However, more recent research shows that these vegetables can be consumed, and some even contain powerful nutrients that offer anti-inflammatory benefits.

For example, Lanier R. et al. (2013) published a study in a medical journal showing that potatoes, peppers, tomatoes, and eggplant contain an alkaloid compound with very powerful anti-inflammatory effects. These products may be beneficial and even ideal for anti-inflammatory diets. Some people may be sensitive to these products, but not all of them are inherently inflammatory.

Consider tomatoes, which are part of the nightshade family. Most people believe they are inflammatory because tomatoes, like other nightshades, contain solanine. But aside from the fact that tomatoes don't contain high levels of this chemical, it doesn't have the same effect on all people. While some people may experience inflammatory effects, this may not apply to you. By eliminating tomatoes from your diet, you will lose their high lycopene and vitamin C content, which provide powerful antioxidant and anti-inflammatory properties.

As for tomatoes and other nightshade vegetables, you'll need to be careful after consuming them. If they trigger symptoms of inflammation, then nightshades may not be right for you. Otherwise, you can continue eating them and adding them to your dishes. If nightshade vegetables trigger inflammation in your body; you can skip the ingredients or substitute them. For example, potatoes can be replaced with sweet potatoes, tomatoes with olives (or simply removed from the recipe), or peppers with carrots (you can remove these as well). Remember, you have to find what works best for you as you improve your health through the anti-inflammatory diet.

The key to determining whether to eat or avoid these foods is observation. As you eliminate inflammatory foods from your diet, you will begin to see positive changes in your health. As you consume these foods, pay attention to your body to see how you react to them. In addition to these "special foods," there are also some foods that you should only eat in moderation so as not to increase your risk of inflammation. These are:

- Poultry
- Black molasses
- Dried fruits
- Coconut
- Plantain
- Honey
- Fructose
- Black tea
- Salt (when using salt, opt for unrefined varieties)

SATURATED FATS

The anti-inflammatory diet doesn't have to be difficult or restrictive. It has to be easy to follow; thus, you shouldn't deprive yourself of your loved foods, especially at first. Remember, it's always best to get into the diet to allow your body to adjust to the new foods you're introducing and the ones you're gradually becoming disabused of. This is the best way to learn how to make smarter, healthier food choices for the rest of your life!

References:
Lanier RK, Gibson KD, Cohen AE, Varga M. Effects of dietary supplementation with the solanaceae plant alkaloid anatabine on joint pain and stiffness: results from an internet-based survey study. Clin Med Insights Arthritis Musculoskelet Disord. 2013 Oct 21;6:73-84. doi: 10.4137/CMAMD.S13001.

A healthy eating pattern for people includes healthy choices, favorite foods, dining out, and alcohol in moderation (if desired).

Confused on where to start when it comes to grocery shopping or preparing your next meal? I will help you with some simple practice examples before following your 28-day meal plan.

What does a daily meal plan look like?

Here is a general guideline before you work with a registered nutritionist dietician:

NUTRIENTS	ANTI-INFLAMMATORY DIET	DIETARY GUIDELINES	
		Women	Men
Calories	2152	19-25y: 2200 26-50y: 2000 51+y: 1800	19-25y: 2800 26-45y: 2600 46-65y: 2400 65+y: 2200
Carbohydrate (% of calories)	31 %	45-65 %	45-65 %
Total Fat (% of calories)	55 %	20-25 %	20-25 %
Saturated Fat (% of calories)	8%	≤10%	≤ 10%
Trans Fat (% of calories)	0%	N/A	N/A
Protein (% of calories)	14 %	10-35 %	10-35 %
Potassium (mg)	1555	≥ 4,700	≥ 4,700
Sodium (mg)	3317	≤ 2,300	≤ 2,300
Calcium (mg)	833	≥ 1,000	≥ 1,000
Fiber (g)	23	19-30y: 28g 31-50y: 26g 51+y: 22g	19-30y: 34g 31-50y: 31g 51+y: 28g
Vitamin B12 (mcg)	9.3	2.4	2.4
Vitamin D (mcg)	15	15	15

WHAT SHOULD YOUR PLATE LOOK LIKE?

Food Group	Frequency	Portion(s)	Serving Size
Vegetables	Daily	5	200g (Salad leaves 80g)
Nuts and seeds	Daily	3	30g
Fish	Daily	4	150g
Beans and legumes	Daily	4	100g Fresh or 30g Dried
Fruit	Daily	5	150g
Carbohydrates with a low glycemic index (whole bread or rice/pasta)	Daily	3	50g (whole bread) 80g (rice/pasta)
Free-range eggs	Daily	2	60g
Fresh Cheese	Daily	2	100g
Yogurt	Daily	2	125mL
White Meat	Daily	2	100g
Spices (Ginger, curcumin,..)	Daily	4	10g
Sweets	Occasionally	1	100g
Red Meat	Weekly	1	100g
Red Wine	Daily	1	125mL
Extra-virgin Oil	Daily	2-3	10mL

Additional Helpful Tips:
- Drink Mineral water (1.5-2L/day).
- Supplements: Vitamin D (especially if you are not exposed to sunlight every day), fiber, n-3, Vitamin B12.

ood Category	Type of Food	Anti-inflammatory role
Omega 3 (Fatty Acids)	• Fatty fish (salmon, mackerel, tuna) • Chia, flax seeds, walnuts	Reduce inflammation and support functionality
Vitamin D	• Fatty fish salmon, mackerel, tuna) • Fortified food with Vitamin D (dairy products, soy milk, orange juice, and cereals) • Cheese, egg yolks	Involved in biochemical path neces to reduce body inflammation
'itamin A, C, E *Antioxidants* *Seasonings*	• Vitamin A: sweet potatoes, carrots, broccoli, leafy greens (kale, spinach) • Vitamin C: citrus, guava, strawberries, peppers, kiwi, pineapple • Vitamin E: spinach, avocado, almonds, sunflower seeds, butternut squash • Seasonings: garlic, rosemary, cinnamon, turmeric (curry)	Helps control oxidative stress caus exercise and injury
Nitric Oxide d Nitrates	• Celery, beets, and leafy green	Nitrates convert to nitric oxide in body which help increase blood fl helping to reduce inflammation a optimize recovery
nthocyanins: l, blue, and urple food	• Blueberries, cherries, blackberries, cranberries, grapes, eggplant, plums, red or purple skinned potatoes, blood orange, radishes	Helps promote muscle pain, redu soreness and general inflammati
High quality protein	• Fish, eggs, meat, and dairy products	Reduce exercise induced muscle dar thanks to the presence of essenti amino acids (e.g., after bodybuildi activity) and support muscle heal

Before you start remember…

The Anti-inflammatory diet is healthy eating at its best. It provides the ideal balance of unrefined carbohydrates, lean proteins, and healthy fats combined with nutrient-dense, fresh seasonal produce.

These principles are at the base of this book's recipes so that you can cook great-tasting meals for your family and friends. Your food will not just taste delicious but also will be rich in healthy ingredients, putting you on the right path to good health and longevity.

8-WEEK MEAL PLAN

WEEK 1

DAYS	BREAKFAST	LUNCH	DINNER
Day 1	Cranberry and chia pudding	Green salad with basil and cherry dressing	Chicken with fennel and zucchini
Day 2	Breakfast squares with coconut and fruit	Salmon soup	Braised bok choy with shiitake mushrooms
Day 3	Maple cinnamon granola	Chicken stew	Ginger salmon
Day 4	Coconut rice with berries	Avocado Vegetarian wraps	Thai-style beef with coconut milk
Day 5	Pear and kale smoothie	mackerel and beet salad	Chicken with pine nuts
Day 6	Veggie muffins	Moroccan spiced lentil stew	Coconut crusted shrimp
Day 7	Chocolate and blueberry smoothie	Baked cod with mushrooms	Chicken drumsticks

WEEK 2

DAYS	BREAKFAST	LUNCH	DINNER
Day 1	Vanilla crepes (Gluten-free)	Rice soup with peppers	Lentil salad with arugula and citrus fruits
Day 2	Arugula and green tea smoothie	Turkey meatballs	Mackerel with almonds and vegetables
Day 3	Mango green tea smoothie	Radish and tomato salad	Shirataki rice and pork balls
Day 4	Gingered blueberry granola	Asian-style noodle soup	Broccoli and sesame (Stir-fried)
Day 5	Vegetable omelet	Ginger sea bass fillets	Bean enchiladas
Day 6	Vegetarian sandwiches	Avocado & Chicken Tortillas (Gluten-free)	Italian minestrone
Day 7	All-berry and banana pancakes (gluten-free)	Lime and salmon patties	Rosemary chicken

WEEK 3

DAYS	BREAKFAST	LUNCH	DINNER
Day 1	Fruit and seed breakfast bars	RICH Corn and cilantro salad	Ginger chicken cooked with citrus fruits
Day 2	Cranberry and chia pudding	fresh cucumber AND Watermelon salad	Sauteed sardines with mashed cauliflower
Day 3	Breakfast squares with coconut and fruit	Artichoke and fresh mint risotto	Lamb chops with rosemary
Day 4	Maple Cinnamon Granola	Sweet Korean Lentils	Turkey Meatball soup with vegetables
Day 5	Coconut rice with berries	fresh cucumber AND Watermelon salad	Orange and ginger chicken
Day 6	Pear and kale smoothie	Baked crab, mushrooms and asparagus	Coconut artichoke soup with almonds
Day 7	Veggie muffins	Salmon salad	Vegetarian pizza

WEEK 4

DAYS	BREAKFAST	LUNCH	DINNER
Day 1	Chocolate and blueberry smoothie	Tuna salad with ginger	Chicken with mint sauce
Day 2	Vanilla crepes (Gluten-free)	Tofu Sloppy Joes	Chicken with cheese and cauliflower rice
Day 3	Arugula and green tea smoothie	Baked sole with coconut milk	CHARD and tomato soup
Day 4	Mango green tea smoothie	Beet salad with apples	Roasted chicken with herbs
Day 5	Gingered blueberry granola	Vegetable kebabs	Fresh tuna steak and fennel salad
Day 6	Vegetable omelet	Pumpkin soup	Beef and garlic mushrooms
Day 7	Vegetarian sandwiches	Healthy Turkey Sloppy Joes	BBQ chicken stuffed zucchini

WEEK 5

DAYS	BREAKFAST	LUNCH	DINNER
Day 1	Fruit and seed breakfast bars	RICH Corn and cilantro salad	Ginger chicken cooked with citrus fruits
Day 2	Cranberry and chia pudding	fresh cucumber AND Watermelon salad	Sauteed sardines with mashed cauliflower
Day 3	Breakfast squares with coconut and fruit	Artichoke and fresh mint risotto	Lamb chops with rosemary
Day 4	Maple Cinnamon Granola	Sweet Korean Lentils	Turkey Meatball soup with vegetables
Day 5	Gingered blueberry granola	Vegetable kebabs	Fresh tuna steak and fennel salad
Day 6	Vegetarian sandwiches	Avocado & Chicken Tortillas (Gluten-free)	Italian minestrone
Day 7	Coconut rice with berries	fresh cucumber AND Watermelon salad	Orange and ginger chicken

WEEK 6

DAYS	BREAKFAST	LUNCH	DINNER
Day 1	Pear and kale smoothie	mackerel and beet salad	Chicken with pine nuts
Day 2	Arugula and green tea smoothie	Baked sole with coconut milk	CHARD and tomato soup
Day 3	Mango green tea smoothie	Beet salad with apples	Roasted chicken with herbs
Day 4	Gingered blueberry granola	Vegetable kebabs	Fresh tuna steak and fennel salad
Day 5	Coconut rice with berries	fresh cucumber AND Watermelon salad	Orange and ginger chicken
Day 6	Vegetable omelet	Pumpkin soup	Beef and garlic mushrooms
Day 7	Maple Cinnamon Granola	Sweet Korean Lentils	Turkey Meatball soup with vegetables

WEEK 7

DAYS	BREAKFAST	LUNCH	DINNER
Day 1	Fruit and seed breakfast bars	RICH Corn and cilantro salad	Ginger chicken cooked with citrus fruits
Day 2	Pear and kale smoothie	mackerel and beet salad	Chicken with pine nuts
Day 3	Breakfast squares with coconut and fruit	Artichoke and fresh mint risotto	Lamb chops with rosemary
Day 4	Maple Cinnamon Granola	Sweet Korean Lentils	Turkey Meatball soup with vegetables
Day 5	Vanilla crepes (Gluten-free)	Tofu Sloppy Joes	Chicken with cheese and cauliflower rice
Day 6	Pear and kale smoothie	Baked crab, mushrooms and asparagus	Coconut artichoke soup with almonds
Day 7	Vegetarian sandwiches	Avocado & Chicken Tortillas (Gluten-free)	Italian minestrone

WEEK 8

DAYS	BREAKFAST	LUNCH	DINNER
Day 1	Gingered blueberry granola	Vegetable kebabs	Fresh tuna steak and fennel salad
Day 2	Arugula and green tea smoothie	Baked sole with coconut milk	CHARD and tomato soup
Day 3	Vegetable omelet	Pumpkin soup	Beef and garlic mushrooms
Day 4	Mango green tea smoothie	Beet salad with apples	Roasted chicken with herbs
Day 5	Coconut rice with berries	fresh cucumber AND Watermelon salad	Orange and ginger chicken
Day 6	Veggie muffins	Salmon salad	Vegetarian pizza
Day 7	Chocolate and blueberry smoothie	Tuna salad with ginger	Chicken with mint sauce

Lizzy McFields

NOW YOU WILL ASK YOURSELF "WHY BLACK AND WHITE EDITION?"

Unfortunately, we are forced to publish in B&W. Otherwise, the book price would be very high…Nevertheless, we have inserted the QR code at the beginning of every recipe chapter. A simple scan shows the recipes in color (downloadable on every device) to provide the best quality in this situation.

For my books, I focused on an ENVIRONMENTAL-FRIENDLY solution using print-on-demand technology and an interconnected network of printers to ensure my books have the smallest carbon footprint possible. This is possible by using the Amazon service. How does it work? When you place an order, the digital file is sent to the printer closest to the book's final shipping destination. The book will be printed in a few days and delivered.

Waste associated with traditional publishing is approximately 40% of all printed books.
If one 10-inch diameter tree yields around 25 books of 150 pages in one year, about 2.5 million trees became books no one wanted for only one Country. Imagine the number of trees saved every year by using print-on-demand technology.

The paper used by printers is thin paper to save more trees.

I hope you support this choice and will enjoy the book and its content!

Important notice: the downloaded material is covered by copyright too.

BREAKFAST & SMOOTHIES

SCAN ME! RECIPES' COLOR IMAGES

Prep
5 m

Portion
4 Servings

Cook
0 m

Per Serving
Calories 482; Sat Fat 29g; Total Fat: 41g; Protein: 7g; Carbohydrates: 29g; Fiber 4.5g; Ca 58mg; K 515mg; Na 25mg

CRANBERRY AND CHIA PUDDING

. . . .

2 ¼ cups coconut milk
¾ cup chia seeds
½ cup hemp seeds
½ cup dried cranberries
¼ cup maple syrup

Directions:

1. Mix chia seeds, hemp seeds, coconut milk, cranberries, and maple syrup in a medium bowl. Cover the bowl and place in the refrigerator overnight.
2. In the morning, stir and serve.

Ingredient Tip: You can replace coconut milk with almond milk.

Prep
15 m

Portion
6 Makes

Cook
30 m

Per Serving
Calories 528; Sat Fat 5g; Total Fat: 42g; Protein: 18g; Carbohydrates: 29g; Fiber 8.8g; Ca 117mg; K 601mg; Na 98mg

FRUIT AND SEED BREAKFAST BARS

. . . .

½ cup pitted dates
¾ cup roasted sunflower seeds
¾ cup of toasted pumpkin seeds
¾ cup white sesame seeds
½ cup dried blueberries
½ cup dried cherries
¼ cup flax seeds
½ cup of almond butter

Directions:

1. Preheat the oven to 325°F (165°C).
2. Line an 8-by-8-inch baking pan with baking paper.
3. In a food processor, chop the dates until reduced to a paste.
4. Add the sunflower seeds, pumpkin seeds, sesame seeds, blueberries, cherries, and flax seeds and blend. Pour the mixture into a medium bowl.
5. Stir in the almond butter. Transfer the mixture to the prepared dish and press firmly.
6. Bake for about 30 minutes, or until the mixture is firm and golden brown.
7. Cool for about 1 hour until it is at room temperature. Remove from pan and cut into 12 squares.
8. Store in refrigerator in a sealed container for up to 1 week.

Substitution Tip: Blueberries can be replaced by raspberry.

BREAKFAST SQUARES WITH COCONUT AND FRUIT

. . . .

6 tbsp coconut oil, melted
2 tbsp coconut sugar
1 cup 4 of honey
2 tbsp ground cinnamon
1 tsp ground ginger
1 tsp ground nutmeg
1 tsp baking soda
1/2 ripe banana, mashed
2 tbsp collagen peptide powder
1 cup cassava flour
1 cup tiger nut flour
2 large free-range eggs
1 cup fresh raspberries

Directions

1.   Cover a large baking pan with wax paper and preheat the oven to 350°F, with the rack in the center of the oven.

2.   Place the melted coconut oil, coconut sugar, honey, cinnamon, ginger, and nutmeg in a large bowl. Beat with a whisk until all ingredients are well combined. Stir in the baking soda, banana, collagen peptide powder, cassava flour, and tiger nut flour until well combined.

3.   Beat the free-range eggs. Gently incorporate the raspberries into the mixture.

4.   Using an offset spatula, pour the batter onto the prepared baking sheet—level the batter into an even layer.

5.   Place the pan in the oven for 16-20 minutes, or until the top is golden brown and the batter is fully cooked.

6.   Place the pan on the counter for 1-2 hours, or until completely cooled. Slice 12 bars, serve and enjoy!

How to Store Tip: Bars can be frozen for up to two months or stored in the pantry in an airtight container for no more than 3 days.

Substitution Tip: tiger nut flour can be substituted by almond flour.

Prep	Portion	Cook
5 m	12 makes	20 m

Per Serving

Calories 220; Sat Fat 6g; Total Fat: 8g; Protein: 1g; Carbohydrates: 39 g; Fiber 1.6g; Ca 16mg; K 116mg; Na 111mg

PEAR AND KALE SMOOTHIE

. . . .

3 cups of kale
1/4 cup cilantro leaves
2 pears, peeled and chopped
2 cups sugar-free apple juice
1 tbsp grated ginger
1 cup crushed ice

Directions:

1.   Place the cabbage, cilantro, pears, apple juice, ginger, and ice in a food processor and blend until smooth. Serve.

Substitution tip: Pears can be substituted with apricots in the summertime.

Prep	Portion	Cook
5 m	2 Servings	0 m

Per Serving

Calories 292; Sat Fat 5g; Total Fat: 9g; Protein: 4g; Carbohydrates: 51g; Fiber 6.4g; Ca 144mg; K 583mg; Na 52mg

COCONUT RICE WITH BERRIES

Prep 10 m
Portion 4 Servings
Cook 30 m

Per Serving
Calories 283; Sat Fat 1g; Total Fat: 3.5g; Protein: 6g; Carbohydrates: 57g; Fiber 4.4g; Ca 102mg; K 343mg; Na 646mg

. . . .

11 cup of brown basmati rice
1 cup of water
1 cup of coconut milk
1 tsp salt
2 dates, pitted and chopped
1 cup fresh blueberries or raspberries, divided in half
¼ cup toasted slivered almonds, split
½ cup flaked coconut, divided

Directions:
1. In a medium saucepan over high heat, combine the basmati rice, water, coconut milk, salt, and date pieces.
2. Stir until the mixture comes to a boil. Reduce the heat to low and cook for 20 to 30 minutes, without stirring, or until the rice is tender.
3. Divide the rice among four bowls and top each serving with ¼ cup blueberries, 1 tbsp almonds, and 2 tbsp coconut.
Substitution tip: Blueberries can be replaced by cherries (pitted).

MAPLE CINNAMON GRANOLA

Prep 15 m
Portion 8 Servings
Cook 40 m

Per Serving
Calories 439; Sat Fat 13g; Total Fat: 30g; Protein: 14g; Carbohydrates: 50g; Fiber g; Ca 73mg; K 479mg; Na 7mg

. . . .

4 cups gluten-free oats
1½ cups sunflower seeds
½ cup maple syrup
½ cup coconut oil
1½ tsp ground cinnamon

Directions
1. Preheat the oven to 325°F (165°C).
2. Line two baking sheets with baking paper.
3. Mix together the oats, sunflower seeds, maple syrup, coconut oil, and cinnamon in a large bowl. Mix well so that the oats and seeds are evenly coated with syrup, oil, and cinnamon.
4. Divide the granola mixture evenly between the two slabs.
5. Place the slabs in the preheated oven and bake for 35-40 minutes, stirring every 10 minutes to brown everything evenly.
6. Cool completely, then store in large glass jars with airtight lids.

Recipe Tip: You can add blueberries to add more flavor.

Prep
5 m

Portion
6 Makes

Cook
20 m

Per Serving
Calories 104; Sat Fat 3g; Total Fat: 8g; Protein: 5g; Carbohydrates: 4g; Fiber 1.2g; Ca 57mg; K 57mg; Na 1179mg

VEGGIE MUFFINS

. . . .

10 large free-range eggs
1 tbsp sea salt
3 tbsp white pepper
2 tbsp fresh chives, chopped
2 tbsp fresh parsley, chopped
2 tbsp fresh basil leaves, finely chopped
1 cup broccoli florets, chopped

Directions

1.   Thoroughly grease a 12-serving muffin pan with oil, or place 12 silicone cupcake liners in the holders. This is important because free-range eggs tend to stick during baking, so be sure to use liners or oil the pan thoroughly. A regular baking spray may not prevent the muffins from sticking. Preheat the oven to 350°F, with the rack in the center of the oven.

2.   Crack the free-range eggs into a large bowl and beat them with the salt and pepper until frothy. Add the chopped chives, parsley, and basil leaves.

3.   Divide the chopped broccoli among the prepared ramekins, about 1 tbsp of broccoli per ramekin.

4.   Carefully pour the egg mixture over the broccoli in the baking dish, leaving about half an inch on top.

5.   Place the baking dish in the oven for about 20 minutes, or until the egg is completely set and the top is lightly browned.

Place the pan on the counter to cool before pouring the muffins onto a serving plate. You may need to use a rubber spatula to dislodge the muffins from the pan. Serve immediately.

Substitution tip: Broccoli can be substituted with fennel.

CHOCOLATE AND BLUEBERRY SMOOTHIE

. . . .

2 cups of regular rice milk
1 cup frozen wild blueberries
2 tbsp of cocoa powder
½ tsp stevia
¼ tsp turmeric
1 cup crushed ice

Directions:

1.   Place rice milk, blueberries, cocoa powder, stevia, turmeric, and ice in a food processor and blend until smooth. Serve immediately.

Substitution tip: Blueberries can be replaced by raspberry.

Prep
5 m

Portion
2 Servings

Cook
0 m

Per Serving
Calories 871; Sat Fat 5g; Total Fat:10g; Protein: 16g; Carbohydrates: 177g; Fiber 10.4g; Ca 155mg; K 535mg; Na 44mg

Prep
5 m

Makes
2 Servings

Cook
10 m

Per Serving
Calories 603; Sat Fat 27g; Total Fat: 39g;
Protein: 18g; Carbohydrates: 50g; Fiber 7.7g; Ca
84mg; K 541mg; Na 114mg

VANILLA CREPES (GLUTEN-FREE)

· ·

2 free-range eggs
1 tsp vanilla
½ cup of nut milk
½ cup water
1 tsp maple syrup
1 cup gluten-free whole wheat flour
2 tbsp coconut oil

Directions:

1. In a medium-sized bowl, combine the eggs,
vanilla, nut milk, water, and syrup until smooth.

Add the flour to the mixture and beat to make a
smooth paste.
2. Take 2 tbsp of coconut oil and melt it in a frying
pan over medium heat.
3. Add ½ crepe batter and tilt and swirl the pan to
form a round crepe.
4. Cook for about 2 minutes until the bottom turns
light brown and pulls away from the pan with a
spatula.
5. Turn it over and cook for another 2 minutes.
6. Serve and repeat with the rest of the batter.

Ingredient tip: If you don't like coconut, you can
replace it with avocado oil or extra-virgin oil. .

Prep
3 m

Portion
1 Servings

Cook
0 m

Per Serving
Calories 347; Sat Fat 7g; Total Fat: 13g; Protein: 11g;
Carbohydrates: 52g; Fiber 13.5g; Ca 478mg; K 711mg; Na
115mg

ARUGULA AND GREEN TEA SMOOTHIE

· · · · · · · · · · · · · ·

1 green tea bag
1 cup of almond milk
3 ice cubes
1 tbsp chia seeds
1 cup frozen arugula
¼ cup frozen blueberries
½ sliced banana
½ tbsp ground cinnamon
1 tsp nutmeg

Direction:

1.   Microwave the almond milk at high
temperature in a large cup or microwave-safe bowl,
stirring at regular intervals to prevent the milk from

boiling. When the milk is boiling, add the tea bag
and let it steep until it reaches the desired strength.
2.   Once the tea has partially cooled, place ice
cubes in the tea.
3.   Meanwhile, add the chia seeds, arugula,
blueberries, banana, cinnamon, and nutmeg in a
high-speed food processor.
4.   Pour the warm tea over the ingredients in
the food processor and process on high speed for 1
minute until smooth.
5.   Serve and enjoy.

Substitution tip: Blueberries can be replaced by
raspberry.

Prep
2 m

Portion
2 Servings

Cook
0 m

Per Serving
Calories 505; Sat Fat g;
Total Fat: 17g; Protein: 30g;
Carbohydrates: 60g; Fiber
4.8g; Ca 330mg; K 1078mg; Na
154mg

MANGO GREEN TEA SMOOTHIE

1 cup crushed ice

. . . .

1 tbsp chopped fresh mint
2 cups mango, diced
2 tbsp turmeric powder
2 tbsp green tea powder
2 cups almond milk
2 tbsp of honey

Directions:
Place the mint, mango, turmeric, green tea, almond milk, honey, and ice in a blender and blend until smooth. Serve.
Substitution Tip: Mango can be substituted with apricots

Prep
10 m

Portion
1 Serving

Cook
15 m

Per Serving
Calories 648; Sat Fat 3g; Total Fat: 28g; Protein: 8g;
Carbohydrates: 99g; Fiber 6.4g; Ca 217mg; K 487mg; Na
441mg

GINGERED BLUEBERRY GRANOLA

. . . .

1-inch fresh ginger, finely grated
1/3 tsp ground cinnamon
1/3 tsp ground nutmeg
1/4 tsp kosher salt
2 tbsp chia seeds
1 cup lightly toasted almond slivers
3 cups gluten-free oats
1 tsp pure vanilla essence
1/3 cup extra-virgin oil
1 2 cups maple syrup
2 cups fresh blueberries
Plain Greek yogurt or soy milk for serving (optional)

Directions:
1. Cover a large baking sheet with wax paper and preheat the oven to 325°F, with the rack in the center of the oven.
2. Place the ginger, cinnamon, nutmeg, salt, chia seeds, almond slivers, and oats in a large bowl. Stir with a wooden spoon to combine.
3. Whisk together the vanilla, sunflower oil, and syrup in a separate medium-sized bowl.
4. Pour the syrup mixture into the bowl of oats and spices, stirring to combine.
5. Gently add fresh blueberries until evenly distributed.
6. Pour the mixture onto the prepared baking sheet and use the wooden spoon to distribute it evenly.
7. Place the baking sheet in the oven for 20 minutes, then stir and turn the granola. Return the pan to the oven for another 20 minutes. The edges of the granola should be lightly browned. Keep an eye on the granola, as it tends to burn quickly.
8. Allow cooling completely before serving or storing.

Substitution Tip: Serve granola with yogurt or soy milk.

Prep
10 m

Portion
2 Servings

Cook
25 m

Per Serving
Calories 335; Sat Fat 6g; Total Fat: 26g;
Protein: 19g; Carbohydrates: 5g; Fiber
1.8g; Ca 118mg; K 489mg; Na 207mg

VEGETARIAN OMELET

. . . .

1 tbsp coconut oil or extra virgin olive oil
4 free-range eggs
1 sweet potato, peeled and
1 zucchini, peeled and sliced
2 tsp of parsley
1 tsp ground black pepper

Directions:

1. Preheat the grill to medium heat.
2. Heat oil in a skillet under the grill until hot.
3. Spread the potato slices on the skillet and cook for 8-10 minutes or until soft.
4. Add the zucchini to the skillet and cook for another 5 minutes.
5. Meanwhile, beat the eggs and parsley in a separate bowl and season with pepper before pouring the mixture over the vegetables in the skillet.
6. Cook for 10 minutes on low heat until golden brown.
7. Remove and turn out onto a plate or cutting board.

Prep
10 m

Portion
4 Servings

Cook
30 m

Per Serving
Calories 409; Sat Fat 6g; Total Fat: 23g;
Protein: 16g; Carbohydrates: 39g; Fiber
8g; Ca 275mg; K 707mg; Na 760mg

VEGETARIAN SANDWICHES

. . . .

2 tbsp extra-virgin olive oil
½ lb sliced champignon mushrooms
Pinch of Sea salt and pepper to taste
1 ripe avocado, sliced
2 tbsp lemon juice
½ tbsp maple syrup
8 slices of grain-free whole wheat bread
4 oz sliced parmesan cheese

Directions:

1. Heat olive oil in a medium skillet over medium heat and saute mushrooms until softened, 5 minutes—season with salt and black pepper. Turn off the heat.

2. Preheat a sandwich press over medium heat 3-5 minutes.
3. Mash avocado in a medium bowl and stir in lemon juice and maple syrup.
4. Spread the mixture on 4 slices of bread, and spread the mushrooms and Parmesan cheese on top.
5. Cover with the other slices of bread and brush the top with olive oil. Grill the sandwiches in the heated press until golden brown, and the cheese is melted.
6. Serve and enjoy!

Substitution Tip: Mushrooms can be replaced by broccoli or zucchini.

Prep	Portion	Cook	Per Serving
7 m	2 Serving	5 m	Calories 646; Sat Fat 8g; Total Fat: 14g; Protein: 9g; Carbohydrates: 135g; Fiber 14.8g; Ca 77mg; K 1817mg; Na 654mg

SHAKSHUKA IN CRUSTY BREAD

. . . .

1 medium orange, squeezed
1 cup cherries, pitted
1 cup strawberries, peeled and sliced
1 cup blueberries
1 tsp baking soda
2 large free-range eggs, beaten
2 bananas, mashed
1 tbsp coconut oil

Directions:

1.   In a small saucepan over medium-high heat, whisk together the orange juice and the three cups of berries. When the juice starts to boil, turn the heat down to medium-low and simmer the fruit for 10-12 minutes. Stir at regular intervals and partially break up the fruit. When the juice thickens, transfer the pot to a wooden cutting board and let cool. The sauce will become thicker as the mixture cools.

2.   Meanwhile, whisk together the baking soda, eggs, and mashed bananas in a medium-sized bowl.

3.   Heat the coconut oil in a large skillet over medium-high heat. When the oil is hot, pour one cup of batter into the pan. Fry the pancake for 4 to 5 minutes, or until the center, is well cooked and the edges are golden brown. Turn the pancake over and fry for another 1 to 2 minutes. Remove the pancake to a plate and keep it warm while you repeat the process with the remaining batter.

4.   Divide the pancakes between two plates and top with the cooled berry sauce before serving.

SIDES & SALADS

SCAN ME! RECIPES' COLOR IMAGES

GREEN SALAD WITH BASIL AND CHERRY DRESSING

Prep
10 m

Portion
4

Cook
0 m

Per Serving
Calories 106; Sat Fat 0g; Total Fat:6g; Protein: 2g; Carbohydrates: 131g; Fiber 3.4g; Ca 46mg; K 126mg; Na 325mg

. . . .

¼ cup extra-virgin olive oil
½ cup pitted cherries
2 tbsp lemon juice
2 tbsp honey
1 tbsp chopped fresh basil
A pinch of sea salt to taste
5 oz blanched broccoli florets
2 cups mixed greens salad

1 cup of snow peas
½ cucumber, sliced
2 green onions, thinly sliced

Directions:
1.   Combine the cherries, olive oil, lemon juice, honey, salt, and basil in a food processor and blend until smooth.
2.   Add the broccoli, mixed greens, peas, cucumber, and green onions to a salad bowl.
3.   Top with the dressing.
Substitution Tip: Broccoli can be substituted with fennel.

MACKEREL AND BEET SALAD

. . . .

1 cup sweet potatoes, peeled
12 ounces (340 g) smoked mackerel fillets, skinned
2 green onions, finely sliced
1 cup cooked beets, cut into wedges
2 tbsp finely chopped dill
2 tbsp extra-virgin olive oil
Juice of 1 lemon, zest of half a lemon
1 tsp cumin seeds, crushed with pestle and mortar
Pinch of black pepper

Directions:
1.   Place potatoes in a small saucepan of boiling water and cook for 15 minutes over medium-high heat or until tender to the fork.
2.   Cool and cut into thick slices.
3.   Place the flaked mackerel in a bowl and add the cooled potatoes, green onions, beet, and dill.
4.   Whisk together the olive oil, lemon juice, cumin seeds, and black pepper in a separate bowl.
5.   Pour over the salad and mix well to coat.
6.   Scatter over the lemon zest.

Recipe Tip: Add mint leaves to add more flavor.
Tip: : Pack into plastic containers and refrigerate, or enjoy immediately.

Prep
5 m

Portion
4

Cook
15 m

Per Serving
Calories 287; Sat Fat 3g; Total Fat:16g; Protein: 23g; Carbohydrates: 13g; Fiber 2.8g; Ca 96mg; K 639mg; Na 246mg

Prep
5 m

Portion
5

Cook
40 m

Per Serving
Calories 20; Sat Fat 0g; Total Fat:0g; Protein: 1g; Carbohydrates: 4g; Fiber 0.7g; Ca 68mg; K 161mg; Na 764mg

LENTIL SALAD WITH ARUGULA

· ·

4 cups vegetable broth
2 cups green lentils
Store-bought citrus vinaigrette
10 cups fresh arugula
1 cup 4 of fresh dill, chopped

Directions:

1. Mix the broth and lentils in a large pot over high heat. When broth begins to boil, reduce heat to medium-low. Simmer the lentils, stirring at regular intervals, until tender and most of the broth has reduced, about 25 to 30 minutes.

2. Transfer the pot to a wooden cutting board and stir in the citrus dressing. Set aside to marinate while you prepare the rest of the dish.

3. Divide the arugula among 5 serving bowls and top with the citrus-covered lentils. Garnish with the dill and serve.

Conservation Tip: To thaw, leave the lentils in the fridge overnight and heat it on the stove for 2-3 minutes before serving with fresh salad.

Prep
15 m

Portion
4

Cook
0 m

Per Serving
Calories 61; Sat Fat 0.7g; Total Fat: 6g; Protein: 1g; Carbohydrates: 1g; Fiber 0.3g; Ca 7mg; K 80mg; Na 119mg

RADISH AND TOMATO SALAD

· ·

2 tomatoes, sliced
6 small red radishes, sliced
2 1/2 tbsp white wine vinegar
½ tbsp chopped chervil
Sea salt and pepper to taste
¼ cup extra-virgin olive oil

Directions:

1. Mix the tomatoes and radishes in a bowl. Set aside.

2. Whisk vinegar, chervil, salt, and pepper in another bowl until blended. Pour over the salad and toss to coat. Serve.

Substitution Tip: Use lemon juice instead of vinegar.

Per Serving
Calories 279; Sat Fat 1g; Total Fat:11g; Protein: g;
Carbohydrates: 42g; Fiber 8g; Ca 48mg; K 386mg;
Na 286mg

FRUIT SALAD

. . . .

4 cups chopped mixed vegetables
1 cup fresh sliced peaches
1 cup fresh cherries, pitted and cut in half
½ cup chopped pecans
¼ cup thinly sliced red onion
¼ cup fresh basil leaves
⅓ cup extra virgin olive oil
¼ cup balsamic vinegar
1 tbsp freshly squeezed lemon juice
½ tbsp honey

A pinch of salt
Freshly ground black pepper, to taste

Directions:
1. In a large bowl, gently combine the greens, peaches, cherries, nectarines, pecans, red onion, and basil.
2. Add the olive oil, vinegar, lemon juice, honey, and salt, season with pepper, and whisk to combine in a small bowl.
3. Pour the dressing over the salad and toss gently. Serve immediately.

Recipe Tip: Add almond and other nuts.

Per Serving
Calories 1197; Sat Fat 6g; Total Fat:24g;
Protein: 66g; Carbohydrates: 187g; Fiber 18g;
Ca 478mg; K 855mg; Na 992mg

RICH CORN AND CILANTRO SALAD

. . . .

2 tbsp roasted, unsalted pumpkin seeds
1⁄4 cup fresh Mexican cheese, crumbled
2 tbsp fresh cilantro leaves, chopped
2 ¾ cup canned black beans, no salt added
1⁄2 cup fresh corn kernels
1⁄2 cup cherry tomatoes, cut in half
6 cups romaine hearts (lettuce), cut into small pieces
1 tsp ground cumin
1/2 tsp sea salt
Freshly ground black pepper to taste
1 tbsp raw honey
2 tbsp fresh lime juice
4 tbsp extra virgin olive oil

Directions
1.   Mix pumpkin seeds, Mexican cheese, cilantro leaves, black turtle beans, corn kernels, tomatoes, and lettuce in a large bowl.
2.   In a small glass bowl, whisk together the cumin, salt, pepper, honey, lime juice, and olive oil.
3.   Pour the dressing over the salad and toss to coat. Serve immediately.

Substitution Tip: Mexican cheese can be replaced by mozzarella cheese.

Prep
25 m

Portion
4

Cook
0 m

Per Serving
Calories 201; Sat Fat 1g; Total Fat:12g; Protein: 2g; Carbohydrates: 24g; Fiber 1.3g; Ca 32mg; K 315mg; Na 529mg

FRESH CUCUMBER AND WATERMELON SALAD

. . . .

Dressing:
½ cup extra-virgin olive oil
¼ cup apple cider vinegar
2 tbsp raw honey
1 tsp fresh grated lemon zest (optional)
Pinch of sea salt
Salad:
4 cups (½ inch) cubed watermelon
1 cucumber, cut into ½-inch cubes
1 cup snow peas, cut in half
1 green onion, white and green parts, chopped

2 cups shredded kale
1 tbsp chopped fresh cilantro

Directions:
Prepare the dressing:
1. In a small bowl, whisk EVO oil, cider vinegar, honey, and lemon zest (if using). Season with sea salt and set aside.
Prepare the salad:
1.   Bring together the watermelon, cucumber, peas, shallots, and dressing in a large bowl.
2.   Divide the kale among four plates and top with the watermelon mixture.
3.   Serve garnishing with cilantro.

Substitution Tip: Watermelon can be replaced by melon or apple.

Prep
5 m

Portion
4

Cook
5 m

Per Serving
Calories 476; Sat Fat 4g; Total Fat: 28g; Protein: 28g; Carbohydrates: 30g; Fiber 10g; Ca 360mg; K 972mg; Na 951mg

SALMON SALAD

. . . .

2 salmon fillets, dried
½ tsp Kosher salt
1 tbsp sunflower oil
1 tbsp crushed garlic
2 tbsp balsamic vinegar
¼ cup extra virgin olive oil
Freshly ground black pepper
4 cups of mixed salad greens
¼ cup thinly sliced red radishes
¼ cup pitted brown olives
1 cup thinly sliced red onion
1 cup and 4 diced cucumbers

Directions:
1.   Season the salmon fillets on both sides with a generous pinch of salt.
2.   In a large skillet over medium heat, heat the sunflower oil. When the oil is hot, fry the salmon for 3-4 minutes per side.
3.   Whisk together the garlic and vinegar in a small glass bowl. Gradually add the olive oil while whisking. If desired, taste the dressing and add a pinch of salt and pepper.
4.   Divide the mixed salad, radish slices, olives, sliced onion, and cucumber into two serving bowls. In each salad bowl, add a fried salmon fillet. Season the contents of the bowls with the dressing and serve.
Ingredient Tip: Replace salmon with tuna.

Prep
5 m

Portion
1

Cook
6 m

Per Serving
Calories 565; Sat Fat 6g; Total Fat:44g;
Protein: 10g; Carbohydrates: 39g; Fiber 13.3g;
Ca 179mg; K 755mg; Na 973mg

TUNA SALAD WITH GINGER

. . . .

2 tbsp grated fresh ginger
2 tbsp crushed garlic
2 tbsp lemon juice
2 tbsp extra virgin olive oil (divided)
1 cup of coconut amino
1 slice of tuna steak
½ avocado, pitted, peeled, and diced
1 English cucumber, diced
1 cup purple cabbage, shredded
1/4 tsp sea salt
Freshly ground black pepper

Directions:
1.   In a medium bowl, whisk together the ginger,
garlic, lemon juice, 1 tbsp olive oil, and coconut

amino acid. Divide the marinade between 2 airtight
containers. Dip the steak into one of the containers.
Close both containers and chill for 10 minutes.
2.   After 10 minutes, remove the container with the
tuna and pour out the marinade. Dry the steak with
paper towels.
3.   Heat the remaining olive oil in a large skillet
over medium heat. When the oil is hot, sear the
steak for 2-3 minutes per side. If you prefer well-
cooked tuna, you can fry it for a few more minutes.
4.   In a salad bowl, mix the avocado, cucumber,
and cabbage. Season with salt and pepper before
drizzling with the reserved and cooled dressing.
Arrange the blanched tuna on top of the salad and
serve.

Ingredient Tip: Replace tuna with cod.

Prep
10 m

Portion
4

Cook
0 m

Per Serving
Calories 109; Sat Fat 0g; Total Fat:3g;
Protein: 2g; Carbohydrates: 21g; Fiber
4.4g; Ca 48mg; K 362mg; Na 287mg

BEET SALAD WITH APPLES

. . . .

2 tbsp extra-virgin olive oil
Juice of 1 lemon
½ shredded beet
1/3 tsp Sea salt to taste
2 apples peeled and julienned
4 cups shredded red cabbage

Directions
1.   Mix the EVO oil, lemon juice, beet, and salt in a bowl. In another bowl, combine the apples and
cabbage.
2.   Pour in the vinaigrette and stir to coat everything. Serve immediately.

Ingredient Tip: Replace apple with pears.

Prep
25 m

Portion
4

Cook
0 m

SWISS CHARD SALAD WITH CHOPPED EGG

. . . .

Dressing:
¼ cup extra-virgin olive oil
3 tbsp freshly squeezed lemon juice
2 tsp raw honey
1 tsp Dijon mustard
1/3 tsp Sea salt, to taste
Salad:
5 cups chopped Swiss chard
3 large hard-boiled eggs, peeled and chopped
1 English cucumber, diced
½ cup sliced radishes

½ cup chopped pecans

Directions:
For the dressing:
1.   Whisk olive oil, lemon juice, honey, and mustard in a small bowl. Season with salt and set aside.
For the salad:
1.   In a large bowl, toss together the chard and dressing for about 4 minutes, or until the greens soften.
2.   Divide the chard evenly among four plates.
3.   Top each salad with the egg, cucumber, radishes, and pecans.

Ingredient tip: *.add more type of nuts.*

Prep
10 m

Portion
2

Cook
0 m

QUICK & EASY HAZELNUT AND PEAR SALAD

. . . .

¼ cup chopped hazelnuts
4 pears, peeled and chopped
2 tbsp honey
2 tbsp balsamic vinegar
2 tbsp extra virgin olive oil
Directions
Combine pears and hazelnuts in a salad bowl. Drizzle with honey, balsamic vinegar, and olive oil. Serve.

Substitution tip: *Pears can be substituted by apples.*

Ingredient Tip: *Add some dark chocolate (chopped).*

Prep
5 m

Portion
1

Cook
5 m

Per Serving
Calories 725; Sat Fat g; Total Fat: 31g; Protein: 49g; Carbohydrates: 71g; Fiber 18g; Ca 249mg; K 913mg; Na 916mg

CORIANDER SHRIMP SALAD

. . . .

6 oz. shrimp, peeled and deveined
2 cups of mixed salad
1 spring onion, finely chopped
1 avocado, pitted, peeled and diced
¼ cup store-bought lime vinaigrette
½ cup chopped cilantro leaves
1/3 tsp sea salt
Freshly ground black pepper

Directions:

1.   Bring a small pot of water to a boil over high heat. When the water boils, add the shrimp and cook for 2-3 minutes, until the shrimp redden and the tails curl into a 'C' shape. Immediately submerge the cooked shrimp in a bowl of ice water to stop the cooking process. Transfer the cooled shrimp to a paper towel-lined plate.

2.   In a large bowl, combine the mixed salads, spring onions, avocado, and dried shrimp.

3.   Whisk together the lime vinaigrette and cilantro leaves in a small glass bowl—season to taste with salt and pepper.

4.   Pour the dressing over the salad and toss to coat. Serve immediately and enjoy.

Ingredient Tip: Frozen shrimp should be thawed under fresh water before cooking.

Prep
10 m

Portion
4

Cook
25 m

Per Serving
Calories 322; Sat Fat 4.5g; Total Fat:19g; Protein: 31g; Carbohydrates: 6g; Fiber 2.5g; Ca 42mg; K 561mg; Na 130mg

CUCUMBER AND SPINACH TACO SALAD (TAKE-AWAY)

. . . .

1 tbsp extra-virgin olive oil
2 chicken breasts, skinless, cut into pieces
2 carrots, sliced
½ large onion, chopped
2 tsp cumin seeds
½ avocado, chopped
1 lime, squeezed
½ cucumber, chopped
½ cup fresh spinach washed

Directions:

1.   Heat oil over medium heat in a skillet and cook chicken for 10 to 15 minutes until golden brown and cooked through.

2.   Remove and set aside to cool.

3.   Add the carrots and onion and continue cooking for 5-10 minutes or until soft.

4.   Add the cumin seeds to a separate pan over high heat and toast until brown before crushing them in a pestle and mortar or blender.

5.   Place them in the pan with the vegetables and turn off the heat.

6.   Add the avocado and lime juice to a food processor and blend until creamy.

7.   In a mason or Kilner jar, pour half of the avocado and lime mixture, then the cumin-roasted vegetables, and finally, the chicken.

8.   Top with the cucumbers and spinach and refrigerate for 20 minutes before serving.

Substitution tip: You can replace spinach with salad leaves.

POULTRY

SCAN ME! RECIPES' COLOR IMAGES

Prep
10 m

Servings
4

Cook
8 m

Per Serving
Calories 872; Sat Fat 10g; Total Fat: 60g;
Protein: 66g; Carbohydrates: 18g; Fiber 3g;
Ca 73mg; K 841mg; Na 342mg

CHICKEN WITH PINE NUTS

4 boneless, skinless chicken breasts
1⁄4 tsp sea salt (divided)
1 tsp white pepper (divided)
3 tbsp avocado oil (divided)
1⁄3 cup fresh basil leaves
2 chopped spring onions (green part only)
1 1⁄2 tbsp freshly squeezed lemon juice
1⁄3 cup lightly toasted pine nuts

Directions:

1.   Place the chicken breasts on a wooden cutting board and, using a wooden mallet, crush and flatten them until they are about 3⁄4 inch thick. Season the breasts with half the salt and half the pepper.

2.   In a large skillet over medium-high heat, heat 1 tbsp of oil. When the oil is hot, tilt the skillet to spread the oil. Add the chicken breasts to the hot oil and fry them for 8 minutes, turning them halfway through cooking. The chicken should be well cooked and no longer pink in the center. Transfer the cooked chicken to a plate.

3.   In a blender, chop the basil leaves, spring onions, lemon juice, pine nuts, and remaining salt and pepper until finely blended. Add the rest of the oil and blend until all the ingredients are well combined.

Cut the chicken against the grain and serve with the pine nut.

Tip: Add some rosemary to add more flavor.

Prep
10 m

Portion
6

Cook
35 m

Per Serving
Calories 305; Sat Fat 4g; Total Fat: 20g;
Protein: 24g; Carbohydrates: 7g; Fiber 1g;
Ca 28mg; K 419mg; Na 723mg

CHICKEN DRUMSTICKS

6 chicken drumsticks
1 cup unsweetened coconut yogurt
½ cup extra virgin olive oil
Juice of 2 limes
2 crushed garlic cloves
1 tbsp raw honey
1 tsp salt
1 tsp ground cumin
½ tsp paprika
½ tsp ground turmeric
¼ tsp freshly ground black pepper
Extra virgin olive oil cooking spray

Directions

1. Place the chicken in a shallow baking dish.
2. In a small bowl, whisk together the yogurt, olive oil, lime juice, garlic, honey, salt, cumin, paprika, turmeric, and pepper until smooth.
3. Pour the yogurt mixture over the chicken. Cover with plastic wrap and chill for 30 minutes or overnight.
4. Preheat the oven to 375°F (190°C).
5. Line a baking sheet with aluminum foil and lightly grease it with cooking spray.
6. Remove the drumsticks from the marinade and place them on the prepared baking sheet. Discard the marinade.
7. Place the baking sheet under the drumsticks and bake for 25 to 35 minutes, or until they begin to brown and are cooked through.

Substitution Tip: paprika can be substituted by grounded ginger.

Prep	Portion	Cook	Per Serving
15 m	4	15 m	Calories 272; Sat Fat 2g; Total Fat:12g; Protein: 27g; Carbohydrates: 17g; Fiber 4.4g; Ca 130mg; K 509mg; Na 790mg

CHICKEN WITH FENNEL AND ZUCCHINI

. . . .

2 tbsp extra virgin olive oil
4 boneless, skinless chicken breasts, cut into strips
1 leek, only the white part, thinly sliced
1 fennel bulb, cut into quarter-inch rounds
3 zucchini, cut into rounds about a foot long.
½ cup chicken broth
1 tsp salt
½ tsp freshly ground black pepper
½ cup sliced green olives
2 tbsp chopped fresh dill

Directions:

1.   In a large skillet over high heat, heat olive oil.
2.   Add the chicken strips. Brown them for 1 to 2 minutes, stirring constantly. Transfer the chicken and its juices to a plate or bowl and set aside.
3.   Add the leek, fennel, and zucchini to the skillet. Sauté for 5 minutes.
4.   Return the chicken and its juices to the pan. Pour in the broth. Add the salt and pepper. Cover the pan and simmer for 5 minutes.
5.   Remove pan from heat and stir in olives and dill.

Prep	Portion	Cook	Per Serving
10 m	4	16 m	Calories 115; Sat Fat 0g; Total Fat:1g; Protein: 2g; Carbohydrates: 25g; Fiber 1g; Ca 44mg; K 189mg; Na 47mg

GINGER CHICKEN COOKED WITH CITRUS FRUITS

. . . .

2 tbsp fresh ginger, finely chopped
2 tbsp crushed garlic
4 tbsp pure maple syrup
2 tbsp gluten-free, low-sodium soy sauce
2/3 cup freshly squeezed orange juice
2 tbsp. freshly grated orange zest
2 oz. boneless, skinned chicken thighs

Directions:

1.   In a large bowl, whisk together the ginger, garlic, syrup, soy sauce, orange juice, and orange zest. Coat the thighs with the orange marinade and let them soak. Cover the bowl with plastic wrap and chill for at least 1 hour.
2.   Line a large rimmed baking pan with foil. Lightly coat the foil with baking spray—Preheat the oven with the rack in the center of the oven.
3.   Place the marinated chicken thighs on the prepared baking sheet, saving the marinade for later. Grill the thighs for 16 minutes, turning them halfway through cooking or until the thighs are cooked through.
4.   Meanwhile, reheat the marinade in a small saucepan over medium-high heat. When the sauce starts to simmer, stir for 1 minute or until the sauce thickens.
5.   Plate the chicken and serve hot with the citrus sauce spread on top.

Ingredient tip: You can replace chicken with turkey.

Prep
13 m

Portion
4

Cook
25 m

Per Serving
Calories 1052; Sat Fat 25g; Total Fat:74g;
Protein: 51g; Carbohydrates: 45g; Fiber 3.2g;
Ca 154mg; K 712mg; Na 679mg

TURKEY MEATBALLS

Meatballs:
1 lb. ground turkey
1 tsp white pepper
1/2 tsp sea salt
1 tsp onion powder
1 1/2 tbsp garlic powder
2 tbsp fresh rosemary, chopped
1 tbsp fresh thyme, chopped
3 tbsp fresh sage, chopped
2 tbsp coconut flour
1 cup 4 of tapioca flour
1 large free-range egg
1 tbsp extra-virgin olive oil

Spinach sauce:
3 tbsp coconut oil
1 tbsp tapioca flour
2 cups chicken broth
1/4 tbsp sea salt
1 tsp white pepper
1 tbsp French mustard
2 tbsp coconut aminos
6 cups fresh spinach
Mashed potatoes for serving (optional)

Directions

1.   *In a large bowl, combine the turkey, pepper, salt, onion powder, garlic powder, rosemary, thyme, sage, coconut flour, tapioca flour, and egg. Use a wooden spoon to mix the ingredients until well combined. Using a small ice cream scoop or clean hands lightly dusted with coconut flour, form the mixture into 20 balls about the same size.*

2.   *In a frying pan over medium heat, heat olive oil. When the oil is hot, fry the meatballs for 3 minutes per side until the meat is well cooked and the outside is golden brown. Transfer the cooked meatballs to a bowl lined with paper towels and keep warm.*

3.   *Add the coconut oil to the same pan over medium-low heat. While the oil melts, whisk together the tapioca flour and chicken broth in a large bowl. Pour the broth into the skillet for 3-4 minutes or until the sauce thickens. Add the salt, pepper, mustard, and coconut aminos to the skillet, whisking to combine. Stir in the spinach for a minute or two or until the leaves wilt.*

4.   *Add the meatballs to the sauce and stir until they are all covered by the sauce and heated through.*

If desired, serve the meatballs and sauce on a bed of creamy mashed potatoes.

Recipe Tip: *You can add rosemary to the recipe to add more taste.*

Prep
10 m

Portion
4

Cook
15 m

Per Serving
Calories 681; Sat Fat 9g; Total Fat: 27g;
Protein: 25g; Carbohydrates: 86g; Fiber
9g; Ca 325mg; K 708mg; Na 923mg

AVOCADO & CHICKEN TORTILLAS (GLUTEN-FREE)

1 lb. boneless, skinless chicken breasts
3⁄8 tsp. sea salt (divided)
2 tsp of all-purpose taco seasoning
1⁄2 cup of low-sodium chicken broth
2 tbsp chopped shallots
1 ripe avocado, chopped
1 cup cherry tomatoes, cut into quarters
2 tbsp balsamic vinegar
1 tbsp extra virgin olive oil
8 corn tortillas (gluten-free), warmed, to serve
1⁄4 cup crumbled feta cheese
Fresh cilantro leaves, chopped, for garnish

Directions:

1. Season chicken breasts with 1/4 tsp salt and taco seasoning. Massage the spices into the meat.

2. In a medium-sized pot over medium heat, bring the broth and seasoned chicken breasts to a light boil. Reduce the heat to maintain a gentle boil and cook the chicken for 15 minutes with the lid on the pot, or until the chicken is well cooked.

3. In a medium-sized bowl, saute the scallions, avocado, and tomatoes together. Whisk together the balsamic vinegar, remaining salt, and olive oil in a small glass bowl. Pour the vinegar over the salsa, stirring to coat. Chill for 1 hour.

4. When the chicken is cooked, transfer it to a wooden cutting board and let it cool for a few minutes. Shred the breasts with a knife and fork when the chicken is cool enough to handle. Divide the shredded chicken among the warmed tortillas. Top with the cooled salsa, then the feta, and garnish with cilantro leaves before serving.

Substitution Tip: You can replace feta cheese with goat cheese.

ROSEMARY CHICKEN

Prep
10 m

Portion
4

Cook
20 m

Per Serving
Calories 353; Sat Fat 5g; Total Fat:22g; Protein: 35g; Carbohydrates: 0g; Fiber 0g; Ca 22mg; K 380mg; Na 398mg

· ·

1½ pounds (680 g) of chicken breast
2 tbsp of extra virgin olive oil
2 tbsp chopped fresh rosemary leaves
½ tsp of sea salt
⅛ tsp freshly ground black pepper

Directions

1. Preheat the oven to 425°F (220°C).
2. Place the chicken slices on a rimmed baking sheet. Brush with olive oil and sprinkle with rosemary, salt, and pepper.
3. Bake for 15-20 minutes, or until juices run clear.

Ingredient tip: You can add turmeric powder or ginger powder.

CHICKEN WITH MINT SAUCE

Prep
20 m

Portion
6

Cook
20 m

Per Serving
Calories 447; Sat Fat 6g; Total Fat:30g; Protein: 47g; Carbohydrates: 18g; Fiber 0.6g; Ca 16mg; K 588mg; Na 1424mg

· ·

Mint sauce:
1 bunch of fresh mint, stem
½ cup extra virgin olive oil
1 clove of garlic
2 tsp lemon zest
½ tsp salt
Pinch of freshly ground black pepper
Chicken:
6 boneless, skinless chicken breasts, cut into 1½- to 2-inch cubes
¼ cup extra-virgin olive oil
¼ cup freshly squeezed lemon juice
1 tsp salt
¼ tsp freshly ground black pepper
A pinch of ground turmeric
2 sprigs of fresh mint

Directions

Prepare the mint sauce:

1.   In a blender or food processor, combine the mint, olive oil, garlic, lemon zest, salt, and pepper. Blend until smooth. 2. Store in the refrigerator in an airtight container for no more than four to five days.

Prepare the chicken:

1.   Soak 12 wooden skewers (6 inches) in water for at least 30 minutes so that the skewers do not burn during grilling.
2.   Combine the chicken, olive oil, lemon juice, salt, pepper, turmeric, and mint in a large zip-lock plastic bag. Close the bag, place it in the refrigerator, turn to coat the chicken, and let it marinate for at least 30 minutes or overnight.
3.   Preheat the grill or place a kitchen grill on high heat.
4.   Thread 3 or 4 chicken cubes onto each skewer. Discard the marinade and mint sprigs.
5.   Reduce the grill to medium heat. Grill chicken for 15 to 20 minutes, occasionally turning, until each skewer is scored on both sides and the chicken is cooked through.
6.   Serve with the mint sauce.

Ingredient tip: Mint can be replaced with basil for the sauce.

Prep	Portion	Cook	Per Serving
20 m	4	28 m	Calories 398; Sat Fat 1g; Total Fat:5g; Protein: 6g; Carbohydrates: 89g; Fiber 2g; Ca 43mg; K 551mg; Na 166mg

ORANGE AND GINGER CHICKEN

4 boneless, skinless chicken breasts, cut into 1-inch pieces
1/2 cup arrowroot starch
2 tbsp extra virgin olive oil
1 tsp fresh ginger, grated
2 tbsp crushed garlic
2 tbsp coconut amino
2 tbsp apple cider vinegar
1 cup raw honey
1 cup freshly squeezed orange juice
Zest of 1 orange
2 cups cauliflower rice
2 spring onions, chopped, for garnish

Directions:

1.   In a large bowl, sauté chicken pieces in arrowroot starch until all pieces are evenly coated.

2.   Heat olive oil in a large skillet over medium heat. When the oil is hot, sauté the ginger and garlic for about 3 minutes, or until fragrant. Gently add the coconut amino, vinegar, honey, orange juice, and zest. Bring the sauce to a gentle simmer and blend for 10 minutes.

3.   Add the chicken and cook for 15 minutes, or until the chicken is well cooked, stirring everything together.

4.   Meanwhile, cook cauliflower rice in a steamer basket over a pot of rapidly boiling water for 5 minutes or until just softened. The water should not touch the bottom of the basket.

5.   Plate the cooked chicken on a bed of steamed cauliflower rice, with the sauce spread all over. Garnish with the spring onions before serving.

Prep
8 m

Portion
8

Cook
30 m

Per Serving
Calories 326; Sat Fat 7g;
Total Fat:25g; Protein: 13g;
Carbohydrates: 13g; Fiber 2g; Ca
40mg; K 290mg; Na 340mg

BBQ CHICKEN STUFFED ZUCCHINI

4 medium zucchini, cut in half lengthwise
1/4 tbsp sea salt
1 tbsp garlic powder
1 tbsp onion powder
1 tbsp smoked sweet paprika
1 tbsp of tomato paste
1 tbsp French mustard
3 tbsp honey
1/3 cup apple cider vinegar
14.5 ounces canned tomato sauce
1 tbsp extra virgin olive oil
1/2 small shallot, diced
2 tbsp crushed garlic
1 lb. cooked chicken, cut into pieces

Directions:

1. Preheat the oven to 400°F, with the metal rack in the center of the oven, and line a large rimmed baking sheet with baking spray.

2. Remove the center of the zucchini cut in half with a metal spoon, leaving about an inch of flesh inside. Lightly coat the inside of the boats with baking spray.

3. In a small glass bowl, whisk together 1 tsp salt, garlic powder, onion powder, paprika, tomato paste, mustard, honey, apple cider vinegar, and tomato sauce.

4. Heat the olive oil in a large frying pan over medium heat. When the oil is hot, add the shallots and sauté for 3 to 5 minutes, or until translucent. Add the garlic and continue sautéing for another 1 to 2 minutes to blend the flavors. Scrape the cooked shallots and garlic into a large bowl and stir-fry the chicken.

5. Pour the BBQ sauce into the bowl of chicken, leaving about 3-4 tbsp aside. Gently stir the chicken until the sauce is evenly distributed.

6. Spread the chicken into the prepared zucchini halves in even amounts. Pour the remaining sauce over the chicken. Bake the pan in the oven for 20-25 minutes or until the zucchini can be easily pierced with a fork.

7. Serve hot and enjoy.

Substitution tip: You can replace chicken with turkey.

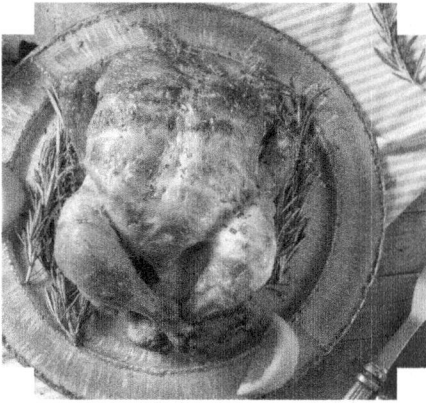

Prep	Portion	Cook	Per Serving
15 m	4	1h 30 m	Calories 366; Sat Fat 3g; Total Fat:13g; Protein: 47g; Carbohydrates: 10g; Fiber 1.5g; Ca 65mg; K 726mg; Na 381mg

ROASTED CHICKEN WITH HERBS

1 whole chicken (4 pounds / 1.8 kg), rinsed and dried
2 lemons, cut in half
1 sweet onion, cut into quarters
4 cloves of garlic, crushed
6 sprigs fresh thyme
6 sprigs fresh rosemary
3 bay leaves
2 tbsp extra-virgin olive oil
1/3 tsp sea salt, to taste
Freshly ground black pepper, to taste

Directions:
1. Preheat the oven to 400°F (205°C). Place the chicken in a roasting pan
2. Place the lemons, onion, garlic, thyme, rosemary, and bay leaves in the cavity. Brush the chicken with olive oil and season lightly with sea salt and pepper.
3. Roast the chicken for about 1 1/2 hours until golden brown and cooked through.
4. Remove the chicken from the oven and let it rest for 10 minutes.
5. Remove the lemons, onion, and herbs from the cavity and serve.

Prep	Portion	Cook	Per Serving
15 m	6	4-6 h	Calories 425; Sat Fat 9g; Total Fat: 36g; Protein: 16g; Carbohydrates: 9g; Fiber 1.5g; Ca 48mg; K 390mg; Na 271mg

HEALTHY TURKEY SLOPPY JOES

½ tsp of sea salt
½ tsp dried oregano

1 tbsp extra virgin olive oil
1 pound (454 g) ground turkey
1 celery stalk, chopped
1 carrot, chopped
½ medium sweet onion, diced
½ red bell pepper, finely chopped
6 tbsp tomato paste
2 tbsp apple cider vinegar
1 tbsp maple syrup
1 tsp Dijon mustard
1 tsp chili powder
½ tsp of garlic powder

Directions:
1. In the slow cooker, combine the olive oil, turkey, celery, carrot, onion, red bell pepper, tomato paste, vinegar, maple syrup, mustard, chili powder, garlic powder, salt, and oregano. Using a large spoon, break the turkey into smaller pieces as you combine it with the other ingredients. Cover the pot and set the temperature to low
2. Cook for 4-6 hours, stir thoroughly and serve.

Ingredient Tip: You can add some mayonnaise to add more taste.

Prep
20 m

Portion
4

Cook
20 m

Per Serving
Calories 372; Sat Fat 5g;
Total Fat:16g; Protein: 13g;
Carbohydrates: 43g; Fiber 0g; Ca
162mg; K 236mg; Na 635mg

GLAZED TURKEY FILLETS WITH CRANBERRIES

. . . .

4 turkey tenderloins
1 tsp garlic powder
1 tsp kosher salt
1 cup 4 of coconut sugar
2 tbsp balsamic vinegar
2 tbsp freshly squeezed orange juice
2 tbsp (filtered) water
2 tbsp maple syrup
1 cup fresh cranberries
Mashed cauliflower, cooked, to serve

Directions:

1. Cover a large baking dish with a border of wax paper and preheat the oven to 400°F, with the rack in the center of the oven.
2. Place the turkey on the prepared baking sheet and sprinkle all the fillets with the garlic powder and salt. Massage the spices over each fillet in an even layer—Bake in the oven for 20 minutes.
3. Whisk the coconut sugar, vinegar, orange juice, water, syrup, and cranberries in a small saucepan over medium heat. When the sauce starts to boil, stir the mixture for 10 minutes. Pour the hot sauce into a high-powered food processor and blend quickly until the sauce is lump-free. You may want to put a kitchen towel on the food processor before blending, as the sauce will be very hot.
4. Plate the baked turkey fillets on a bed of cooked cauliflower puree, topped with the cranberry glaze. Serve warm.

Prep
8 m

Portion
4

Cook
31 m

Per Serving
Calories 465; Sat Fat 10g; Total Fat:27g; Protein: 22g; Carbohydrates: 34g; Fiber 4g; Ca 372mg; K 550mg; Na 782mg

CHICKEN WITH CHEESE AND CAULIFLOWER RICE

. . . .

2 tbsp extra virgin olive oil
2 tbsp crushed garlic
1 small shallot, diced
4 cups broccoli florets
1 lb. boneless, skinless chicken breasts, cut into 1-inch cubes
2 cups cauliflower rice
1 ½ cups store-bought cheese sauce

Directions:

1. Preheat the oven to 350°F, with the rack in the center of the oven.
2. Heat olive oil in a large ovenproof skillet over medium heat. When the oil is hot, sauté the garlic and scallions for 4 to 5 minutes, or until the scallions soften. Add the broccoli florets for another 5 minutes. Add the chicken cubes and saute for 5 minutes, or until the chicken is well cooked. Add the rice to the cauliflower for 2-3 minutes.
3. Pour the cheese sauce into the pan and stir until everything is evenly coated, and the sauce is hot.
4. Transfer the pan to the oven and bake for 15 minutes. Serve hot and enjoy!

Substitution tip: You can replace cheese sauce with mushroom sauce.

FISH & SEAFOOD

SCAN ME! RECIPES' COLOR IMAGES

Prep	Portion	Cook	Per Serving
10 m	4	15 m	Calories 682; Sat Fat 6g; Total Fat: 31g; Protein: 34g; Carbohydrates: 67g; Fiber g; Ca 92mg; K 763mg; Na 501mg

SALMON SOUP

. . . .

¼ cup extra virgin olive oil

1 red bell pepper, chopped

1 pound (454 g) skinless, boneless salmon, cut into half-inch pieces

2 cans of crushed tomatoes (28 ounces / 794 g), 1 drained and 1 undrained

6 cups chicken broth without added salt

2 cups diced sweet potatoes

1 tsp of onion powder

½ tsp of sea salt

¼ tsp freshly ground black pepper

Directions:

1.   In a large pot over medium-high heat, heat olive oil until shimmering.

2.   Add the red bell pepper and salmon. Cook for about 5 minutes, occasionally stirring, until the fish is opaque and the bell pepper is soft.

3.   Add the tomatoes, chicken broth, sweet potatoes, onion powder, salt, and pepper.

4.   Bring to a boil and reduce heat to medium. Cook for about 10 minutes, occasionally stirring, until the sweet potatoes are soft.

Prep 5 m **Portion** 8 **Cook** 10 m

Per Serving
Calories 719; Sat Fat 2g; Total Fat:17g; Protein: 18g; Carbohydrates: 173g; Fiber 4.4g; Ca 642mg; K 563mg; Na 924mg

GINGER SALMON

. . . .

1 fillet of wild salmon with skin on, dried
1 tbsp sea salt
2 tbsp coconut amino (plus 2 tbsp)
2 tbsp grated fresh ginger (divided)
3 tbsp extra virgin olive oil (divided)
3 tbsp crushed garlic
2 kg baby bok choy, cut in half lengthwise

Directions:

1.   Place the salmon fillet on a wooden cutting board and season both sides with salt.
2.   In a medium-sized bowl, whisk together coconut aminos and 1 tsp of fresh ginger. Spread the seasoned salmon with the mixture and cover the bowl with plastic wrap. Chill for 20 minutes.
3.   Heat 2 tsp of olive oil in a large skillet over

medium-high heat. When the oil is hot, add the remaining ginger and garlic and sauté for 2 minutes. Add the remaining coconut aminos and the bok choy. Sauté the bok choy in the skillet for another 2 minutes, or until the leaves crisp up. Pour the contents of the pan into a large bowl and keep warm.

4.   Return the skillet to the heat and add the remaining olive oil. Over medium heat, fry the salmon with the skin side down for 6 minutes. Save the marinade. Keep an eye on the heat to prevent the salmon from burning.

5.   After 6 minutes, turn the fish over and add the marinade to the pan. Cook the fish for another 2 minutes, or until it is well cooked and opaque.

6.   Spread the cooked bok choy into two serving bowls and top with the salmon. Pour the pan juices over all bowls and serve.

Ingredient tip: *You can use onion to replace garlic.*

Prep 10 m **Portion** 4 **Cook** 6 m

Per Serving
Calories 319; Sat Fat 2g; Total Fat:27g; Protein: 6g; Carbohydrates: 16g; Fiber 1.8g; Ca 48mg; K 364mg; Na 421mg

COCONUT CRUSTED SHRIMP

. . . .

2 free-range eggs
1 cup unsweetened dry coconut
¼ cup coconut flour
½ tsp sea salt
¼ tsp paprika
Pinch of cayenne pepper
Pinch of freshly ground black pepper
¼ cup coconut oil
1 lb (454 g) of raw, shelled, and peeled shrimp

Directions

1.   In a small shallow bowl, beat the eggs.

2.   Mix coconut, coconut flour, salt, paprika, cayenne pepper, and black pepper in another small shallow bowl.
3.   In a large skillet over medium-high heat, heat the coconut oil.
4.   Pat the shrimp dry with a paper towel.
5.   Working one at a time, hold each shrimp by the tail, dip it into the egg mixture, and then into the coconut mixture until coated. Place in the hot skillet. Cook 1 to 3 minutes per side. Transfer to a paper towel-lined plate to drain excess oil.
6.   Serve immediately.

Ingredient tip: *You can replace coconut flour with almond flour.*

Prep	Portion	Cook	Per Serving
10 m	4	30 m	Calories 606; Sat Fat 3g; Total Fat:26g; Protein: 62g; Carbohydrates: 31g; Fiber 4.4g; Ca 211mg; K 908mg; Na 1174mg

MACKEREL WITH ALMONDS AND VEGETABLES

. . . .

1 medium butternut squash, peeled and cut into thin strips
3 1/2 cups chopped broccoli florets
2 large carrots, peeled and thinly sliced
2 tbsp avocado oil
1 1/2 tbsp sea salt (divided)
1 tsp freshly ground black pepper
1 tsp garlic powder
3 ¾ cups almond flour
1 cup tapioca flour
1 tsp dried dill
1 tsp smoked sweet paprika
1 cup raw unsalted almonds
2 large eggs
4 mackerel fillets, blotted and dried
1 lemon, cut into 4 wedges

Directions:

1.   Cover a large baking dish with a border of foil and preheat the oven to 425°F, with the rack in the center of the oven.
2.   Mix the squash, broccoli, and carrots in a large bowl. Add the oil, 1 tsp salt, pepper, and garlic powder, stirring until all vegetables are evenly coated. Fan out the coated vegetables in a single layer on the prepared baking sheet. Place the baking sheet in the oven for 20 minutes.
3.   In a medium bowl, whisk together the almond flour, tapioca flour, dill, paprika, and remaining ½ tsp salt. Place the almonds in a high-speed blender and process at high speed for 20 to 30 seconds until the almonds resemble coarse sand. Pour the almonds into a second bowl. Lightly beat the eggs in a third bowl.
4.   After 20 minutes, remove the baking dish from the oven. Remove the vegetables and push them to the sides of the baking dish to make room for the fillets.
5.   Line up the three bowls next to the baking sheet, starting with the flour and ending with the almonds. Start by tossing 1 mackerel fillet in the flour, then the eggs, and finally the almonds. Place the fillet on the baking sheet and repeat with the others. Spread the remaining almonds over the fillets and gently press them onto the coated fish.
6.   Place the baking sheet in the oven for 11 to 13 minutes, or until the fish flakes when pricked with a fork and the vegetables are soft.
Serve immediately, with the lemon wedges on the side.

Suggestion Tip: mackerel fillets can be replaced by cod.

Prep	Portion	Cook	Per Serving
10 m	2	10 m	Calories 204; Sat Fat 1g; Total Fat:9g; Protein: 25g; Carbohydrates: 4g; Fiber1 g; Ca 33mg; K 455mg; Na 92mg

GINGER SEA BASS FILLETS

. . . .

2 sea bass fillets
1 tsp black pepper
1 tbsp extra virgin olive oil
1 tsp ginger, peeled and chopped
1 clove of garlic, thinly sliced
1 red chili pepper, seeded and thinly sliced
2 green onion stalks, sliced

Directions:

1. Take a frying pan and heat the oil over medium-high heat.
2. Sprinkle the sea bass with black pepper and score the fish's skin a few times with a sharp knife.
3. Add the sea bass fillet to the hot skillet with the skin side down.
4. Cook for 5 minutes and turn.
5. Cook for another 2 minutes.
6. Remove the sea bass from the skillet and let it rest.
7. Add the chili, garlic, and ginger and cook for about 2 minutes or until golden brown.
8. Remove from heat and add the green onions.
9. Spread the vegetables over the sea bass and serve.

Ingredient tip: You can remove chili from the recipe if you have intestinal irritation from hot spiced meals.

Prep	Portion	Cook	Per Serving
10 m	4	15 m	Calories 158; Sat Fat 2g; Total Fat:14g; Protein: 3g; Carbohydrates: 7g; Fiber 3g; Ca 61mg; K 479mg; Na 196mg

SAUTÉED SARDINES WITH MASHED CAULIFLOWER

. . . .

2 heads of cauliflower, divided into large florets
4 tbsp extra-virgin olive oil, divided by two
¼ tsp salt
4-ounce (113 g) cans of sardines in water, drained
1 cup fresh parsley, finely chopped

Directions:

1. Fill a large pot with 2 inches of water and insert a steamer basket. Bring the water to a boil over high heat.
2. Add the cauliflower to the basket. Cover and steam for 8-10 minutes, or until florets are tender. Transfer the cauliflower to a food processor.
3. Add 2 tbsp of olive oil and salt to the cauliflower. Process the cauliflower until smooth and creamy. Depending on the size of the food processor, you may need to do this in two stages.
4. In a medium-sized bowl, coarsely mash the sardines.
5. Add the remaining 2 tbsp of olive oil to a medium skillet over low heat. When the oil shimmers, add the sardines and parsley. Cook for 3 minutes. The sardines should be hot, not boiling.
6. Serve the sardines with a generous portion of mashed cauliflower.

Ingredient Tip: sardines can be replaced by mackerel.

Prep
20 m

Portion
4

Cook
10 m

Per Serving
Calories 202; Sat Fat 2g; Total Fat: 11g; Protein: 20g; Carbohydrates: 6g; Fiber 1g; Ca 64mg; K 476mg; Na 234mg

LIME AND SALMON PATTIES

. . . .

8 oz (227 g) boneless salmon fillet cooked and cut into slivers
2 eggs
¾ cup almond flour, more if needed
1 shallot, white and green parts, minced
Juice of 2 limes (2 to 4 tbsp), plus more if needed
Zest of 2 limes (optional)
1 tbsp chopped fresh dill
¼ tsp sea salt
1 tbsp extra-virgin olive oil
1   lime, cut into wedges

Directions:

1.   Mix the salmon, eggs, almond meal, shallot, lime juice, lime zest (if using), dill, and sea salt in a large bowl until the mixture firms up when pressed.

2.   If the mixture is too dry, add more lime juice; add more almond flour if it is too wet. Divide the salmon mixture into 4 equal portions and form patties about half an inch thick. Place them in the refrigerator for about 30 minutes to firm up.

3.   Place a large skillet over medium-high heat and add the olive oil.

4.   Add the salmon patties and brown them for about 5 minutes per side, turning them once.

5.   Serve the patties with lime wedges

Prep
5 m

Portion
2

Cook
20 m

Per Serving
Calories 372; Sat Fat 2g; Total Fat:16g; Protein: 25g; Carbohydrates: 47g; Fiber 23.6g; Ca 306mg; K 907mg; Na 1066mg

BAKED CRAB, MUSHROOMS AND ASPARAGUS

. . . .

4 oz. crabmeat or jumbo crab.
2 tbsp. AIP mayonnaise (vegan)
1⁄8 tbsp garlic powder
2 large Portobello mushrooms, stripped of stems and gills and cleaned
1/3 tsp kosher salt
Freshly ground black pepper
2 tbsp extra virgin olive oil (plus 1 tbsp)
2 kg asparagus, cut off at the ends

Directions:

1.   Preheat the oven to 375°F, with the rack in the center of the oven.

2.   Place the crabmeat, mayonnaise, and garlic powder in a large bowl. Using a wooden spoon, gently stir all the ingredients until the crabmeat is evenly coated. You should not over-mix, as the meat will break down.

3.   Arrange the tops of the cleaned mushrooms on one side of a foil-lined baking sheet. Sprinkle each mushroom lightly with salt and pepper. Pour 1 tsp of oil over each seasoned cap. Pour an equal amount of crab mixture into each hat.

4.   Arrange the asparagus on the other half of the baking dish. Drizzle with remaining oil and season to taste with salt and pepper.

5.   Place baking dish in the oven for 20 minutes, or until asparagus is fork tender.

6.   Plate the crab-stuffed mushrooms alongside the baked asparagus spears and serve hot.

Ingredient Tip: A lobster can replace crabmeat.

FLAVORFUL GARLIC MUSSELS

Prep 5 m	**Portion** 4	**Cook** 35 m	**Per Serving** Calories 762; Sat Fat 18g; Total Fat: 33g; Protein: 66g; Carbohydrates: 48g; Fiber 3g; Ca 459mg; K 942mg; Na 1066mg

2 tbsp coconut oil
2 tbsp grated fresh ginger
2 tbsp crushed garlic
1 shallot, thinly sliced
2 tbsp white wine vinegar
1/3 tsp of kosher salt
1 tbsp fish sauce
2 tbsp coconut amino
2 cups unsweetened whole coconut milk
2 pounds of fresh mussels, cleaned
1 cup 4 of fresh cilantro leaves, chopped
1 spring onion, finely chopped
2 garlic and herb AIP bread rolls (Gluten-free), cut into bread sticks lengthwise

Directions

1. Melt the coconut oil in a large pot over medium heat. When the oil is hot, add ginger, garlic, and scallions. Stir-fry and saute for 3-5 minutes until the scallions become translucent. Add the vinegar for another 2-3 minutes.
2. Add the salt, fish sauce, coconut amino acid, and coconut milk to the pot, stirring to combine.
3. Stir the mussels into the pot, discarding any already been opened. You should never try to cook mussels that have already been opened. Put a lid on the pot and cook the mussels for 5-7 minutes, discarding those that have not opened after a few minutes. If they do not open, it means they are inedible.
4. Pour the cooked mussels into a large serving bowl and toss with the chopped cilantro leaves. Sprinkle with the spring onions and serve with bread on the side for the optional dip.

Substitution tip: Replace mussels with shrimp.

ROSEMARY AND LEMON COD

Prep 10 m	**Portion** 2	**Cook** 10 m	**Per Serving** Calories 290; Sat Fat 1g; Total Fat:7g; Protein: 52g; Carbohydrates: 0g; Fiber 0g; Ca 30mg; K 810mg; Na 932mg

2 tbsp extra virgin olive oil
24oz (680 g) cod, skinned and boned, cut into 4 fillets
1 tbsp chopped fresh rosemary leaves
½ tsp freshly ground black pepper or more to taste
½ tsp sea salt
Juice of 1 lemon

Directions

1. In a large nonstick skillet over medium-high heat, heat olive oil until shimmering. Season the cod with rosemary, pepper, and salt
2. Add the fish to the skillet and cook for 3-5 minutes per side until opaque.
3. Pour lemon juice over cod fillets and cook for 1 minute.

Substitution tip: you can replace cod with sole fish.

Prep
20 m

Portion
4

Cook
20 m

Per Serving
Calories 256; Sat Fat 5g; Total Fat:10g; Protein: 31g; Carbohydrates: 10g; Fiber 1g; Ca 137mg; K 560mg; Na 850mg

BAKED SOLE WITH COCONUT MILK

. . . .

2 tbsp of hot water

A pinch of saffron threads

2 pounds (907 g) of sole fillets

¼ tsp sea salt

2 tbsp freshly squeezed lemon juice

1 tbsp coconut oil

1 sweet onion, chopped, or about 1 cup of pre-cut onion packet

2 tsp bottled minced garlic

1 tsp fresh grated ginger

1 cup canned whole coconut milk

2 tbsp chopped fresh cilantro

Directions

1. Put the water in a small bowl and sprinkle the saffron threads. Let stand for 10 minutes.

2. Preheat the oven to 180°C.

3. Rub the fish with sea salt and lemon juice and place the fillets in a 9-by-9-inch baking dish. Roast the fish for 10 minutes.

4. While the fish is roasting, place a large skillet over medium-high heat and add the coconut oil.

5. Add the onion, garlic, and ginger. Sauté for about 3 minutes, or until softened.

6. Add coconut milk and saffron water. Bring to a boil. Reduce the heat to low and simmer the sauce for 5 minutes. Remove the pan from the heat.

7. Pour the sauce over the fish. Cover and cook for about 10 minutes, or until the fish flakes easily with a fork.

8. Serve the fish with cilantro.

Substitution tip: *sole fish can be replaced by cod.*

Prep
5 m

Portion
2

Cook
5 m

Per Serving
Calories 371; Sat Fat 4g; Total Fat: 31g; Protein: 7g; Carbohydrates: 20g; Fiber 8.8g; Ca 85mg; K 941mg; Na 1116mg

(DECONSTRUCTED) SUSHI TUNA ROLLS

. . . .

2 tbsp fish sauce

2 tbsp coconut amino

2 tbsp fresh ginger, grated

2 tbsp crushed garlic

2 slices of tuna

2 tbsp wasabi paste

3 tbsp mayonnaise (vegan)

1 large Hass avocado, pitted, peeled, and diced

1 English cucumber, cut into small pieces

1 English cucumber, diced

2 tbsp cilantro-lime vinaigrette

1 tbsp extra virgin olive oil

Directions:

1.   In a large bowl, whisk together the fish sauce, coconut amino acid, ginger, and garlic. Coat the tuna steaks with the marinade and let them soak. Cover the bowl with plastic wrap and chill for 25 minutes.

2.   Whisk together the wasabi paste and mayonnaise in a small glass bowl. Chill while preparing the rest of the dish.

3.   Mix the avocado, cucumbers, and vinaigrette in a medium-sized salad bowl. Save for later.

4.   In a large skillet over high heat, heat the olive oil. When the oil is hot, fry the tuna steaks for 2 minutes per side. The outside will cook while the inside will remain pink.

5.   Serve the pan-seared steaks alongside the cooled salad, with a drizzle of wasabi mayonnaise on the side.

Prep
5 m

Portion
4

Cook
40 m

Per Serving
*Calories 611; Sat Fat 4g; Total Fat:22g;
Protein: 65g; Carbohydrates: 41g; Fiber 4.7g;
Ca 92mg; K 811mg; Na 817mg*

SALMON AND VEGETABLES WITH HONEY AND SOY

. . . .

2 tbsp crushed garlic
1 tbsp freshly squeezed lemon juice
1 tbsp raw honey
3 tbsp of extra virgin olive oil
1 1/2 tbsp gluten-free, low-sodium soy sauce
4 salmon fillets with skin on
1 pound sweet potatoes, cut into 1/4-inch cubes
1/4 tbsp sea salt (divided)
1 tsp freshly ground black pepper (divided)
12 oz. fresh sweet potatoes, cut into pieces

Directions:

1.   Cover a large rimmed baking sheet in foil. Coat the tin foil with a light layer of baking spray, and set the oven to preheat to 400°F, with the wire rack in the center of the oven.

2.   In a large bowl, whisk together 1 tsp garlic, lemon juice, honey, 1 tbsp oil, and soy sauce. Coat the salmon fillets with the marinade and set them aside in the marinade bowl.

3.   Place the sweet potato cubes on the prepared baking sheet and toss them with 1 tbsp oil, 1 tsp salt, and 1 tsp pepper. Place the baking dish in the oven for 20 to 25 minutes or until the sweet potatoes soften.

4.   In a medium-sized bowl, sauté the haricot verts with the remaining oil, garlic, salt, and pepper. Add them to the skillet of sweet potatoes and saute everything together. Move the vegetables to the side to make room for the salmon fillets.

5.   Arrange the salmon fillets on half the baking sheet, discarding the remaining marinade. Return the baking sheet to the oven for 15 minutes, or until the vegetables are fork tender and the salmon is well cooked.

6.   Serve warm and enjoy.

Substitution tip: *You can replace salmon with tuna.*

Prep
15 m

Portion
4

Cook
25 m

Per Serving
*Calories 129; Sat Fat 1g; Total Fat:7g;
Protein: 11g; Carbohydrates: 6g; Fiber
2.2g; Ca 49mg; K 369mg; Na 155mg*

FRESH TUNA STEAK AND FENNEL SALAD

. . . .

2 tuna steaks (1 inch)
2 tbsp extra-virgin olive oil, 1 tbsp olive oil for brushing
1 tsp crushed black peppercorns
1 tsp crushed fennel seeds
1 fennel bulb, cut and sliced
½ cup water
1 lemon, squeezed
1 tsp fresh parsley, chopped

Directions

1.   Coat the fish with the oil and then season with the peppercorns and fennel seeds.

2.   Heat the oil over medium heat and sauté the fennel slices for 5 minutes or until light brown.

3.   Add water to the pan and cook for 10 minutes until the fennel is tender.

4.   Add the lemon juice and lower the heat to a simmer.

5.   Meanwhile, heat another skillet and saute tuna steaks for about 2 to 3 minutes per side for medium cooking. (Add 1 minute per side for medium and 2 minutes per side for medium cooking).

6.   Serve the fennel mix with the tuna steaks on top and garnish with fresh parsley.

SNACKS & APPETIZERS

SCAN ME! RECIPES' COLOR IMAGES

Prep
10 m

Makes
4

Cook
35 m

Per Serving
Calories 433; Sat Fat 9g; Total Fat:38g; Protein: 11g; Carbohydrates: 17g; Fiber 4g; Ca 45mg; K 400mg; Na 430mg

SPICED NUT CURRY MIX WITH MAPLE AND BLACK PEPPER

. . . .

1 cup raw cashew nut pieces
½ cup raw macadamia nuts, coarsely chopped
½ cup raw pumpkin seeds
1 tbsp freshly pressed coconut oil
2 tsp maple syrup
2 tsp curry powder
½ tsp kosher salt
¼ tsp freshly ground black pepper
Pinch of cayenne pepper

Directions:

1.   Preheat the oven to 300°F (150°C). Line a baking sheet with baking paper.
2.   Combine cashews, macadamias, and pumpkin seeds in a large bowl
3.   In a medium saucepan over low heat, melt the coconut oil with the maple syrup for about 1 minute. Remove from heat and pour over the nut mixture. Add the curry powder, salt, black pepper, and cayenne pepper and mix well to coat everything. Spread the mixture on the prepared baking sheet.
4.   Bake, stirring once, until the nuts turn light brown, 30 to 35 minutes. Allow cooling on the baking sheet. 5. Store in an airtight container at room temperature for up to 3 days.

Prep
15 m

Portion
4

Cook
30 m

Per Serving
Calories 297; Sat Fat 2g; Total Fat:12g; Protein: 12g; Carbohydrates: 38g; Fiber 6.3g; Ca 180mg; K 603mg; Na 219mg

BREADED BALLS OF SPINACH AND KALE

. . . .

2 cups frozen or fresh spinach, thawed and chopped
1 cup fresh or frozen kale, thawed and drained
½ cup onion, finely chopped
1 clove of garlic, finely chopped
3 tbsp extra virgin olive oil
2 free-range eggs, beaten
½ tsp ground thyme
½ tsp dried rubbed oregano
½ tsp dried rosemary
1 cup dried rice or corn breadcrumbs (gluten free)
½ tsp dried oregano
1 tsp ground black pepper

Directions

1.   Preheat the oven to 180°C.
2.   Line a baking sheet with baking paper.
3.   Mix the olive oil and eggs in a bowl, add the spinach, garlic, and onions, and stir to coat everything.
4.   Add the rest of the ingredients, stirring to combine.
5.   Using the palms of your hands, form one-inch balls and place them on the baking sheet.
6.   Bake for 15 minutes, then turn the balls over.
7.   Continue baking for another 15 minutes or until golden brown.
8.   Serve and enjoy!

Prep
5 m

Portion
4

Cook
10 m

Per Serving
Calories 35; Sat Fat 0g;
Total Fat:1g; Protein: 3g;
Carbohydrates: 3g; Fiber 0g; Ca
23mg; K 123mg; Na 199mg

LEMON GRILLED OYSTERS

. . . .

24 fresh oysters in their shells
¼ tsp sea salt
White pepper
½ lime, squeezed

Directions:
1. Preheat grill to high temperature.
2. With the flatter side against the grill, cook oysters for 5-10 minutes, or until they open.
3. Break off the top half of each shell, leaving the oysters in the bottom half.
4. Transfer the grilled oysters to a serving platter. Season the oysters with salt and pepper. Pour lime juice over the oysters and serve immediately.

Prep
15 m

Portion
2

Cook
0 m

Per Serving
Calories 297; Sat Fat 2g;
Total Fat:15g; Protein: 10g;
Carbohydrates: 33g; Fiber 8.4g;
Ca 68mg; K 216mg; Na 1116mg

CHICKPEA HUMMUS

. . . .

1 (15-ounce) (425 g) can of chickpeas, drained and rinsed
¼ cup extra virgin olive oil
¼ cup fresh lemon juice
¼ cup chopped onion
1 clove of minced garlic
1 tsp of sea salt
½ tsp ground cumin

Directions:
1. In a medium-size bowl, use a potato masher to mash the chickpeas until they are in pieces.
2. Add the olive oil, lemon juice, onion, garlic, salt, and cumin, and continue mashing until you have a lightly crushed paste.
3. Let stand for 30 minutes at room temperature for the flavors to develop, then serve.

Ingredient Tip: add mint leaves for more taste.

Prep	Portion	Cook	Per Serving
5 m	4	0 m	Calories 231; Sat Fat 1g; Total Fat: 13g; Protein: 4g; Carbohydrates: 28g; Fiber 4g; Ca 45mg; K 544mg; Na 35mg

APRICOT BITES

. . . .

1 cup dried apricots, finely chopped
1 cup raw walnuts or pecans, finely chopped
½ cup dried coconut
1 tbsp honey

Directions:

1. Mix ingredients until a sticky dough forms.
2. Form 8 balls with the palms of your hands.
3. Cover and refrigerate for at least 2 hours to set.
4. Serve or wrap for a later time.

Prep	Portion	Cook	Per Serving
5 m	5	10 m	Calories 142; Sat Fat 0g; Total Fat:3g; Protein: 7g; Carbohydrates: 22g; Fiber 7.5g; Ca 55mg; K 391mg; Na 701mg

BLACK BEANS WITH CILANTRO AND LIME

. . . .

1 tbsp extra virgin olive oil
1 whole clove of garlic, crushed
15.5 oz. canned black turtle beans drained and rinsed
1 1/2 tsp. kosher salt
1 tsp white pepper
1 tsp ground cumin
1 lime, squeezed

Directions:

1. Heat olive oil in a small saucepan over medium heat. When the oil is hot, sauté the garlic for 1-3 minutes, or until fragrant and well roasted.
2. Add the beans, salt, pepper, cumin, and lime juice. Cook the beans for 4-6 minutes until well cooked, stirring regularly. If you want to vary the dish's consistency, use a fork to mash some of the beans into the sauce.
3. Allow the beans to cool slightly before serving.

Prep
5 m

Portion
4

Cook
20 m

Per Serving
Calories 438; Sat Fat 7g; Total Fat:34g; Protein: 25g; Carbohydrates: 12g; Fiber 4g; Ca 587mg; K 348mg; Na 1125mg

GREEK-STYLE ALMOND FLATBREAD

1/4 tbsp sea salt (plus 1.8 tbsp)
1/2 tsp baking soda
1/4 cup grated parmesan cheese
1/2 cup blanched almond meal
1 large free-range egg, lightly beaten
2 tbsp almond milk
2 tbsp extra virgin olive oil
2 heirloom tomatoes, thinly sliced
4 oz. mozzarella cheese, grated
3 cups fresh basil leaves, torn
Store-bought balsamic glaze

Directions:

1. *Whisk together 1/2 tsp salt, baking soda, Parmesan cheese, and almond flour in a medium bowl. Whisk in the egg and milk until all ingredients come together. Bring the dough together and knead for 5 minutes until smooth with clean hands. Divide the dough in half and cover with plastic wrap. Chill the dough for 30 minutes or until firm to the touch.*

2. *Preheat the oven to 350°F, with the rack in the center of the oven. Coat a large rimmed baking sheet with cooking spray.*

3. *Once the dough has cooled and firmed to the touch, roll each piece into an oblong shape about 1 inch thick, using greaseproof paper over and under the dough as you roll it out to prevent sticking. Place the dough side by side on the prepared baking sheet and bake for about 13 minutes, or until the edges of the dough begin to crisp up.*

4. *Remove the baking sheet from the oven, and with a basting brush, coat the bread with 1 tsp of oil on each. Arrange the sliced tomatoes on the bread in an even layer and sprinkle the mozzarella cheese, leaving about an inch of bread open around the edge to create a border.*

5. *Place the pan back in the oven for 4 to 6 minutes to melt the cheese. Season the warm bread with the remaining salt. Garnish with fresh basil leaves and balsamic glaze before serving.*

6. *Serve warm.*

PLANTAIN CHIPS

Prep 10 m

Portion 2

Cook 20 m

Per Serving
Calories 767; Sat Fat 4g; Total Fat:28g; Protein: 4g; Carbohydrates: 142g; Fiber 10.6g; Ca 11mg; K 923mg; Na 605mg

. . . .

2 pounds (907 g) plantains, peeled and thinly sliced diagonally
¼ cup extra-virgin olive oil
½ tsp smoked paprika
½ tsp kosher salt

Directions:

1.   Preheat the oven to 375°F (190°C). Line two baking sheets with baking paper. Arrange the plantain slices in a single layer on the prepared baking sheets

2.   Brush the top of the slices with half of the olive oil, then turn them over and brush the other side with oil. Sprinkle with the paprika and salt.

3.   Roast for 18-20 minutes, turning halfway through cooking, until the bananas are golden brown and crisp. Allow to cool completely.

4.   Store in an airtight container at room temperature for up to 3 days.

Ingredient Tip: you can replace plantains with zucchini.

AVOCADO HUMMUS WITH CILANTRO AND LIME

Prep 5 m

Portion 4

Cook 0 m

Per Serving
Calories 324; Sat Fat 2g; Total Fat:17g; Protein: 11g; Carbohydrates: 36g; Fiber 12g; Ca 73mg; K 610mg; Na 305mg

. . . .

3 tbsp water (filtered)
½ tbsp crushed red pepper (optional)
1 tsp freshly ground black pepper
1/2 tsp sea salt
1 tsp ground cumin
1 tbsp crushed garlic
3 tbsp freshly squeezed lime juice
¼ cup fresh coriander leaves, chopped
1 small ripe avocado, pitted and peeled
2 tbsp. extra virgin olive oil
15 oz. canned chickpeas without added salt, drained and rinsed

Directions:

1.   Place all ingredients in a high-power blender and blend at high speed until smooth. You will need to pause occasionally to scrape the walls of the blender.

2.   If the hummus is too thick, add more filtered water, 1 tbsp at a time, until the desired consistency is achieved.

3.   Pour the hummus into a bowl and chill, covered with plastic wrap, until ready to serve.

Prep
5 m

Portion
4

Cook
15 m

Per Serving
Calories 111; Sat Fat 0g; Total Fat:5g; Protein: 3g; Carbohydrates: 17g; Fiber 4.8g; Ca 102mg; K 555mg; Na 733mg

BAKED SPINACH CHIPS

. . . .

2 lb. cabbage spinach
1 tsp kosher salt
3 tbsp extra virgin olive oil

Directions

1.   Preheat the oven to 375°F, with the rack in the center of the oven, and line a large rimmed baking sheet with greaseproof paper.

2.   With a sharp knife, remove the spinach stems and cut the larger leaves to about the same size.

3.   In a large bowl, toss the spinach leaves with the salt and olive oil until all leaves are evenly coated and seasoned.

4.   Place the seasoned spinach on the prepared baking sheet and bake until the leaves are crisp, about 15 minutes.

5.   Allow the chips to cool on the counter before serving.

Per Serving
Calories 432; Sat Fat 5g; Total Fat:39g; Protein: 5g; Carbohydrates: 23g; Fiber 18g; Ca 35mg; K 908mg; Na 407mg

Prep
10 m

Portion
3

Cook
0 m

GUACAMOLE

. . . .

4 medium, ripe avocados, cut in half and pitted
1 tsp onion powder
½ tsp sea salt

Directions

1.   Scoop out the avocado flesh and place in a medium bowl. Add the garlic powder and salt

2.   With a fork, mash the avocado until creamy.

3.   Serve immediately, or cover and refrigerate for up to 2 days.

Prep	Portion	Cook	Per Serving
20 m	4	0 m	Calories 423; Sat Fat 7g; Total Fat: 37g; Protein: 8g; Carbohydrates: 20g; Fiber 2g; Ca 44mg; K 303mg; Na 337mg

CASHEW NUT HUMMUS

. . . .

1 cup raw cashews, soaked in filtered water for 15 minutes and drained
2 cloves of garlic
¼ cup filtered water
1 tbsp of extra virgin olive oil
2 tsp coconut amino
1 tsp freshly squeezed lemon juice
½ tsp ground ginger
¼ tsp sea salt
Pinch of cayenne pepper

Directions

1. In a food processor (or blender), combine the cashews, garlic, water, olive oil, aminos, lemon juice, ginger, salt, and cayenne pepper.
2. Blend until smooth. Use a silicone spatula to scrape down the sides of the food processor bowl, if necessary.
3. Cover and refrigerate before serving, if desired, or store for up to 5 days.

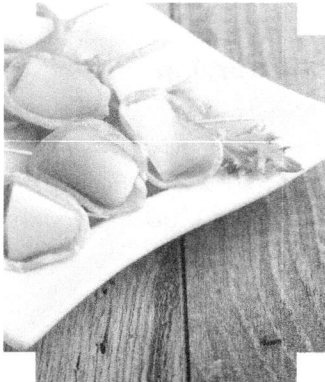

Prep	Portion	Cook	Per Serving
5 m	4	0 m	Calories 48; Sat Fat 0g; Total Fat:1g; Protein: 5g; Carbohydrates: 5g; Fiber 0g; Ca 8mg; K 256mg; Na 375mg

SLICES OF CANTALOUPE WRAPPED IN HAM

. . . .

12 ripe cantaloupe
5 slices of smoked ham
1/2 tsp chopped thyme
1 tsp maple syrup

Directions:

1. Place the melon on a wooden cutting board and remove the rind using a sharp knife. Cut the melon into strips 2 x 2 inches thick.
2. Cut the ham into thin strips and wrap each piece of melon in a strip of ham.
3. Arrange the wrapped cantaloupe slices on a serving platter. Garnish the slices with thyme and drizzle with syrup.
4. Serve and enjoy.

Prep	**Portion**	**Cook**	**Per Serving**
5 m	8	20 m	Calories 221; Sat Fat 2g; Total Fat:22g; Protein: 3g; Carbohydrates: 6g; Fiber 2.7g; Ca 20mg; K 115mg; Na 1309mg

ROSEMARY PECANS COVERED IN HONEY

. . . .

1 tbsp raw honey
1 tbsp sunflower oil
1 tbsp fresh rosemary leaves, finely chopped
2 cups unsalted pecans
1 tsp cayenne pepper
1 1/2 tbsp sea salt

Directions

1.   Cover a large baking sheet with a border of foil. Coat the tin foil with a light layer of baking spray and set the oven to preheat to 325°F, with the wire rack in the center of the oven.

2.   Combine the honey, sunflower oil, and rosemary leaves in a small glass bowl. Microwave at high intensity for 10-second intervals until the mixture reaches the consistency of a drizzle.

3.   Toss pecan halves with the honey mixture in a medium-sized bowl until all nuts are evenly coated.

4.   Fan out the coated pecans onto the prepared baking sheet and sprinkle cayenne pepper and salt in an even layer.

5.   Bake for 20 minutes, or until the coating hardens and the nuts are well toasted.

6.   Cool completely before serving.

SOUPS & STEWS

SCAN ME! RECIPES' COLOR IMAGES

CHICKEN STEW

. . . .

Prep 15 m

Portion 6

Cook 4 h

Per Serving
Calories 640; Sat Fat 13g; Total Fat:29g; Protein:40 g; Carbohydrates: 54g; Fiber 5g; Ca 83mg; K 604mg; Na 1350mg

2 cups chicken broth
1 cup unsweetened coconut milk
¼ cup chopped fresh cilantro (optional)

1 tbsp extra virgin olive oil
3 pounds (1.4 kg) of boneless, skinless chicken thighs
1 large onion, thinly sliced
2 cloves of garlic, thinly sliced
1 tsp chopped fresh ginger
2 tsp ground turmeric
1 tsp whole coriander seeds, lightly crushed
1 tsp salt
¼ tsp freshly ground black pepper

Directions:

1. Pour the oil into a slow cooker.
2. Add the chicken, onion, garlic, ginger root, turmeric, cilantro, salt, pepper, chicken broth, and coconut milk and stir everything together.
3. Cover and cook on high heat for 4 hours. Garnish with chopped cilantro (if using) and serve.

ONION AND MUSHROOM SOUP

. . . .

Prep 5 m

Portion 4

Cook 30 m

Per Serving
Calories 348; Sat Fat 14g; Total Fat: 21g; Protein: 4g; Carbohydrates: 37g; Fiber 2g; Ca 68mg; K 564mg; Na 781mg

2 tbsp extra virgin olive oil
4 tbsp crushed garlic
1 shallot, thinly sliced
4 cups champignon mushrooms, sliced
½ tsp kosher salt
1 whole bay leaf
3 sprigs of fresh thyme
6 cups beef broth
1 cup unsweetened whole coconut milk

Directions:

1. Heat olive oil in a large pot over medium heat.

When the oil is hot, sauté the garlic, scallions, and mushrooms for 10 minutes until the scallions turn translucent, and the mushrooms darken. Add a pinch of salt, bay leaf, thyme, and beef stock. Lower the heat to maintain a gentle simmer. Put a lid on the pot and cook for 20 minutes, stirring at regular intervals to prevent burning.

2. Discard the herbs before adding the coconut milk.
3. Use an immersion blender to puree the soup in the pot.
4. Pour the hot soup into bowls and serve.

Ingredient Tip: Replace coconut milk with almond milk.

Prep
10 m

Portion
6

Cook
25 m

Per Serving
Calories 485; Sat Fat 13g; Total Fat:23g;
Protein: 14g; Carbohydrates: 62g; Fiber 11g;
Ca 214mg; K 819mg; Na 1050mg

MOROCCAN SPICED LENTIL STEW

2 lb. red potatoes, peeled and cut into quarters
3 tbsp avocado oil
2 celery stalks, diced
1 small shallot, diced
3 medium carrots, peeled and diced
4 tbsp crushed garlic
1 tsp white pepper (divided)
2 tbsp kosher salt (divided)
3 tsp ground cinnamon
1 tsp ground turmeric
1 1/2 tbsp ground cumin
2 tbsp smoked sweet paprika
4 cups vegetable broth
1 1/4 cup red lentils
1 cup spinach
2 tbsp freshly squeezed lemon juice
1\2 cup coconut cream
2 tbsp ghee
1 tbsp baking powder
3-5 tbsp almond milk
Fresh coriander leaves, chopped, for garnish

Directions

1.   Place potatoes in a large pot of water and boil over high heat until softened about 15-18 minutes.

2.   While potatoes are boiling, heat avocado oil in a large pot. When the oil is hot, sauté the celery, scallions, and carrots for 5 minutes, or until the scallions are translucent and the carrots begin to soften. Add the garlic for 1 minute so that the flavors blend. Add half the pepper, half the salt, cinnamon, turmeric, cumin, and paprika until all the spices are well incorporated.

3.   Pour the broth into the pot and deglaze the bottom by scraping up any bits of food that have stuck to the bottom of the pot while stirring. Add the lentils and stir. When the stock begins to boil, reduce the heat to medium-low and simmer with the lid for 10 to 12 minutes, or until the lentils soften. Add the spinach and lemon juice, stirring for 2-3 minutes until the spinach has reduced.

4.   When the potatoes are cooked, drain the water in the sink and place the potatoes in a large bowl. Mash them with a fork and mix them with the remaining coconut cream, ghee, salt, and pepper. Add the baking powder and then the almond milk, 1 tbsp at a time, until the desired consistency for the mashed potato is achieved. Serve the stew on a bed of mashed potatoes and garnish with the fresh cilantro leaves.

Ingredient Tip: Replace almond milk with rice or coconut milk.

Prep
15 m

Portion
4

Cook
15 m

Per Serving
Calories 182; Sat Fat 4g;
Total Fat:12g; Protein: 16g;
Carbohydrates: 4g; Fiber 1g; Ca
25mg; K 312mg; Na 275mg

GARLIC LAMB STEW

. . . .

1 pound (454 g) ground lamb
1 tbsp extra virgin olive oil
1 chopped onion
1 tsp dried oregano
½ tsp sea salt
¼ tsp freshly ground black pepper
1 can of chopped tomatoes (28 ounces / 794 g),
drained
5 cloves of garlic, minced

Directions:

1.   In a large nonstick skillet over medium-high heat, cook the lamb for about 5 minutes, crumbling it with a wooden spoon until browned.

2.   Drain the fat and transfer the lamb to a plate. Return the pan to the heat, add the olive oil, and heat it until shimmering.

3.   Add the onion, oregano, salt, and pepper. Cook for 5 minutes, stirring until the onions are soft.

4.   Return the lamb to the skillet and stir in the tomatoes. Cook for 3 minutes, stirring occasionally, or until heated through.

5.   Add the garlic. Cook for 30 seconds, stirring constantly.

Prep
10 m

Portion
8

Cook
5-6 h

Per Serving
Calories 421; Sat Fat 4g;
Total Fat:13g; Protein: 34g;
Carbohydrates: 42g; Fiber 4.3g;
Ca 78mg; K 745mg; Na 500mg

RICE SOUP WITH PEPPERS

. . . .

1 tbsp extra virgin avocado oil
1 small shallot, diced
3 tbsp crushed garlic
4 cups beef stock
1 lb. ground beef
1 1/2 tbsp white pepper
1 tsp kosher salt
1 tsp dried dill
1 tsp dried oregano
1 tsp smoked sweet paprika
2 cups long-grain brown rice
14.5 oz. diced canned tomatoes with juices
14.4 oz. canned tomato sauce
1 green bell pepper, seeded and diced

Directions

1.   In a large skillet over medium-high heat, heat the avocado oil. When oil is hot, sauté scallions for 3-4 minutes or until translucent. Add the garlic for 1-2 minutes so that the flavors blend. Pour in the broth and add the beef, stirring for 3-5 minutes, until the beef is well cooked.

2.   Pour the beef into a large pot and stir in the bell pepper, salt, dill, oregano, paprika, rice, diced tomatoes, tomato sauce, and peppers.

3.   Put the lid on and simmer for 5 to 6 hours.

4.   Pour the soup into bowls and serve hot.

Ingredient Tip: *Replace the beef stock with chicken stock.*

Prep
10 m

Portion
6

Cook
40 m

Per Serving
Calories 462; Sat Fat 10g;
Total Fat:41g; Protein: 15g;
Carbohydrates: 7g; Fiber 1.4g;
Ca 52mg; K 273mg; Na 630mg

TURKEY MEATBALL SOUP WITH VEGETABLES

· · · · · · · · · · · · · · · ·

1 tbsp Dijon mustard
1 lb. ground turkey
1 tsp dried basil
1 tsp garlic powder
½ tsp dried oregano
½ tsp Sea salt and pepper to taste
¼ tsp red pepper flakes
3 tbsp extra virgin olive oil
2 carrots, diced
2 cloves of garlic, minced
1 white onion, diced
½ tsp dried thyme

6 cups vegetable broth
2 cups shredded kale

Directions:

1. Place mustard, ground turkey, basil, garlic powder, oregano, salt, pepper, and red pepper flakes in a bowl. Using your hands, mix the ingredients until well combined—form one-inch balls with the meat mixture.

2. Heat the olive oil in a saucepan over medium heat and sauté the onion, carrots, garlic, and thyme for about 5 minutes, stirring gently.

3. Add the broth and cabbage and bring to a boil. Add the meatballs. Simmer for 15 to 20 minutes until the meatballs are cooked, and the cabbage has softened. Serve.

Ingredient Tip: Replace turkey with chicken.

Prep
5 m

Portion
6

Cook
20 m

Per Serving
Calories 427; Sat Fat 5g; Total Fat:
24g; Protein: 28g; Carbohydrates:
26g; Fiber 3g; Ca 97mg; K 836mg;
Na 1053mg

VIETNAMESE BEEF SOUP

· ·

4 tbsp crushed garlic
1 whole cinnamon stick
6 inches of fresh ginger, peeled and cut in half lengthwise
7 oz. of packaged shirataki noodles
10 cups of beef bone broth
1 cup 4 oz. of fish sauce
2 tbsp. pure maple syrup
1 tsp kosher salt
1 cup and 4 whole Thai basil leaves
1 cup and 4 cilantro leaves, chopped
2 spring onions, finely chopped
1 pound raw porterhouse steak, finely chopped against the grain

1 lime, cut into 6 wedges

Directions

1. Mix the garlic, cinnamon, ginger, noodles, broth, fish sauce, syrup, and salt in a large pot. When the broth starts to boil, reduce the heat to maintain a gentle simmer and cook covered for 20 minutes, stirring at regular intervals.

2. Discard the ginger, cinnamon, and any bits floating on the surface.

3. Divide the basil leaves, cilantro leaves, spring onions, steak, and noodles among 6 serving bowls. Pour the hot soup over all bowls; the steak will cook into the soup.

4. Serve the bowls hot, with the lime wedges on the side.

Prep	Portion	Cook	Per Serving
10 m	4	20 m	Calories 444; Sat Fat 22g; Total Fat:29g; Protein: 5g; Carbohydrates: 47g; Fiber 4g; Ca 64mg; K 405mg; Na 1172mg

ASIAN-STYLE NOODLE SOUP

2 large free-range eggs, chilled

1 tbsp extra virgin olive oil

3 tbsp red curry paste

2 tbsp grated fresh ginger

3 tbsp crushed garlic

2 baby bok choy, separated white and green

2 medium carrots, thinly sliced

1 bell pepper, seeded and diced

4 cups vegetable broth

1 tsp kosher salt

2 tbsp raw honey

1 tbsp coconut amino

13.5 oz. of canned whole coconut milk

4 oz. of packaged vermicelli noodles

1 lime, squeezed

1 cup 4 fresh cilantro leaves, chopped

1 ½ medium red onions, thinly sliced

Directions

1.   Bring 1 inch of filtered water to a boil in a saucepan over high heat. When water begins to boil, add cooled eggs and boil uncovered for 6 minutes. Fill a medium-sized bowl with ice and cold water. After 6 minutes, transfer the hard-boiled eggs to the ice bath and set them aside to cool.

2.   Heat olive oil in a large skillet over medium heat. When the oil is hot, sauté the curry paste, ginger, and garlic for 1-2 minutes, until fragrant. Add the white parts of the bok choy stalks, carrots, and peppers. When the vegetables are well incorporated, pour in the broth. Turn the heat up to medium-high and bring the broth to a boil. Once the broth boils, lower the heat to medium-low and maintain a gentle simmer for 4 minutes until the carrots are soft.

3.   Stir in salt, honey, coconut amino acid, and coconut milk. Add the green parts of the bok choy and cook for 1-2 minutes, or until the leaves are reduced.

4.   Add the noodles and simmer for 3 minutes, stirring, or until the noodles are well cooked.

5.   Peel the cooled eggs and cut them in half.

6.   Serve the noodles garnished with lime juice, cilantro leaves, red onions, and sliced eggs.

Substitution Tip: Replace coconut milk with almond milk and coconut amino with soy sauce.

Prep
10 m

Portion
4

Cook
30 m

Per Serving
Calories 278; Sat Fat 19g;
Total Fat: 25g; Protein: 5g;
Carbohydrates: 15g; Fiber 5.4g;
Ca 42mg; K 144mg; Na 773mg

COCONUT ARTICHOKE SOUP WITH ALMONDS

. . . .

1 tbsp extra virgin olive oil
2 medium shallots, chopped
10 ounces artichoke hearts
3 cups vegetable broth
1 tbsp fresh lemon juice
½ tsp Sea salt
⅛ tsp cayenne pepper
1 cup of plain coconut cream
1 tbsp chopped fresh chives
2 tbsp toasted almonds

Directions

1.   Heat the oil in a saucepan over medium heat. Place shallots and sauté until softened, about 3 minutes. Add the artichokes, broth, lemon juice and salt.
2.   Bring to a boil, lower the heat and simmer for 10 minutes. Add the cayenne pepper.
3.   Transfer to a food processor and blend until pureed. Return to the pot. Combine coconut cream and simmer for 5 minutes.
4.   Top with chives and almonds.

Prep
7 m

Portion
6

Cook
20 m

Per Serving
Calories 345; Sat Fat 5g; Total Fat:25g;
Protein: 8g; Carbohydrates: 27g; Fiber
4.2g; Ca 86mg; K 628mg; Na 1402mg

CHARD AND TOMATO SOUP

. . . .

1 tbsp avocado oil
1 shallot, finely chopped
1 1/2 tbsp sea salt (divided)
6 cups vegetable broth without added salt
1 sprig of fresh rosemary
15 oz. salt-free canned sea beans, drained and rinsed
1 tbsp of tomato paste
26.5 oz. of packed tomatoes
3 tbsp. crushed garlic
2 cups water (filtered)
1 cup 2 whole raw cashews
2 tbsp. balsamic vinegar
1⁄3 cup fresh basil leaves, chopped
2 cups fresh chard

Directions:

1.   In a large pot over medium heat, heat the avocado oil. When oil is hot, sauté shallots for 4 minutes, or until tender. Add a tsp of salt, vegetable broth, rosemary, beans, tomato paste, tomatoes, and garlic. When the soup starts to boil, lower the heat and simmer for 15 minutes, stirring regularly to prevent burning.
2.   Mix the water and cashews in a microwave-safe dish. Heat the cashews in the microwave at high speed for 3 minutes. Discard the water. Stir the heated cashews into the pan.
3.   Discard the fresh herbs before using an immersion blender to puree the soup. Add the remaining salt, vinegar, basil, and herbs, stirring to combine. Cook the soup for 2 minutes, stirring until the chard has reduced.
4.   Pour the soup into bowls and serve hot.

Prep
10 m

Portion
6

Cook
2 h

Per Serving
Calories 18; Sat Fat 0g; Total Fat: 0g; Protein: 1g; Carbohydrates: 4g; Fiber 1.3g; Ca 42mg; K 167mg; Na 339mg

ITALIAN MINESTRONE

1 can of diced tomatoes with juice, 14 ounces
1 can of kidney beans, 14 ounces, well-drained and rinsed
2 stalks of celery, diced
2 carrots, diced
1 zucchini, diced
1 small onion, diced
1 tbsp lemon juice, freshly squeezed
1 tsp sea salt
½ tsp garlic powder
½ tsp dried oregano
½ tsp dried basil leaves
½ tsp dried rosemary
2 bay leaves
6 cups water
1 cup packed fresh spinach

Directions:

1.   Combine the tomatoes, beans, celery, carrots, zucchini, onion, lemon juice, salt, garlic powder, oregano, basil, rosemary, bay leaf, and broth in the slow cooker.

2.   Cover the pot and set the cooking level to low—Cook for 6 to 8 hours.

3.   Remove and discard the bay leaves. Stir in the spinach and let it wilt for 5 minutes before serving.

6.   Cook for 3 minutes until the spinach is wilted. Serve with a garnish of Parmesan cheese.

7.   Enjoy!

Tip: To extract more vitamins from vegetables, add a tbsp of extra-virgin oil and stir the soup before you eat.

Ingredient Tip: To reduce cooking time use a pressure cooker; time will be reduced to 40-50 minutes starting from when the cooker is on pressure.

Prep 5 m

Portion 5

Cook 40 m

Per Serving
Calories 279; Sat Fat 17g; Total Fat: 24g; Protein: 3g; Carbohydrates: 17g; Fiber 4.6g; Ca 64mg; K 573mg; Na 1081mg

CARROT AND TURMERIC GINGER SOUP

. . . .

2 tbsp avocado oil
1 small shallot, diced
1 cup winter squash, cut into cubes
4 medium carrots, cut into small pieces
1 tbsp ground turmeric
1 inch fresh ginger, grated
1/2 tbsp sea salt
1 tsp white pepper
13.5 oz. canned lite coconut milk
3 cups vegetable broth
1/3 cup fresh parsley leaves, chopped

Directions:

1. Heat the oil in a large pot over medium heat. When the oil is hot, sauté the shallots, squash, and carrots until the vegetables are tender and the shallots turn transparent.

2. Stir in the turmeric, ginger, salt, and pepper for 2 minutes, so the flavors blend. Pour in the coconut milk and broth, stirring to combine. When the soup starts to boil, reduce the heat to maintain a gentle simmer and cook covered for 20 minutes. Stir the pot at regular intervals to prevent burning.

3. When all the vegetables are fork-tender, use an immersion blender to puree the soup in the pot.

4. Pour the hot soup into bowls and serve garnished with the parsley leaves.

Prep 5 m

Portion 6

Cook 30 m

Per Serving
Calories 69; Sat Fat 0g; Total Fat: 5g; Protein: 1g; Carbohydrates: 6g; Fiber 1.2g; Ca 17mg; K 168mg; Na 383mg

CAULIFLOWER SOUP

. . . .

1 small white onion, diced
3 cloves of garlic, chopped
1 small celery root, peeled and cut into 1-inch pieces
1 head of cauliflower, chopped
2 tbsp avocado oil
4 cups vegetable broth
2 shallots, sliced

Directions:

1. Heat the avocado oil in a large pot over medium heat and sauté the onion and garlic for 3 minutes.

2. Add the celery root and cauliflower. Increase the heat to medium and continue sautéing for 5 minutes, or until the cauliflower begins to brown and caramelize on the edges.

3. Add the broth and bring to a boil. Reduce heat to medium-low and simmer for 10 minutes. Remove the pot from the heat.

4. With an immersion blender or in batches with a standard blender, puree the soup to a creamy consistency.

5. Serve immediately sprinkled with scallions.

Substitution Tip: You can replace cauliflower with broccoli.

Prep	Portion	Cook	Per Serving
5 m	6	55 m	Calories 96; Sat Fat 0g; Total Fat:3g; Protein: 3g; Carbohydrates: 17g; Fiber 1.6g; Ca 52mg; K 690mg; Na 1231mg

PUMPKIN SOUP

· · · · · · · · · · · · · · · · ·

1 pumpkin, sliced
3 tbsp extra virgin olive oil
1 tbsp sea salt
2 red bell peppers
1 onion, cut in half
1 head of garlic
¼ tsp cayenne pepper
½ tsp ground coriander
½ tsp ground cumin
Roasted pumpkin seeds

Directions:

1. Preheat oven to 350°F. Brush the pumpkin slices with oil and sprinkle with salt. Place pumpkin slices skin side down in greased baking dish; bake for 20 minutes.
2. Brush the onion with oil. Cut off the head of garlic and brush with oil. Add peppers, onion and garlic to squash. Cook for 10 minutes. Cool.
3. Scoop out the pulp from the squash and transfer to a food processor. Coarsely chop the peppers, peel and chop the onion, and remove the garlic cloves from the head.
4. Transfer everything to the food processor and pour in 6 cups of water. Blend the soup until smooth. If it is very thick, add a little water to reach the desired consistency. Sprinkle with salt, cayenne pepper, coriander, and cumin. Serve.

Prep	Portion	Cook	Per Serving
5 m	6	30 m	Calories: 170; Fat: 13.1g; Sat fat: 3.2g; Carb: 9.6g; Fiber: 2.5g; Sugar: 4.5g; Protein: 6g

ZUCCHINI AND BASIL SOUP

· ·

2½ pounds zucchini, chopped
2 tbsp. olive oil
1 medium onion, chopped
4 cloves garlic, minced
⅓ cup fresh basil leaves, chopped
⅓ cup heavy cream
4 cups chicken broth
Salt and black pepper, to taste
2 tbsp. extra virgin olive oil

Directions:

1. In a large skillet over medium-low heat, add olive oil, zucchini, and onion.
2. Cook for about 6 minutes, stirring often.
3. Add the garlic and sauté for about 1 minute.
4. Add the chicken broth and let simmer over medium-high heat.
5. Reduce heat to medium-low and simmer for about 15 minutes.
6. Sprinkle with basil, salt, and black pepper and remove from heat.
7. Blend the soup with an immersion blender until it forms a smooth puree.
8. Ladle the soup into serving bowls and drizzle with extra virgin olive oil.
9. Add the heavy cream and serve immediately.

Ingredient Tip: Serve with slices of toasted whole-wheat bread.

Substitution tip: Vegetable broth can be used instead of chicken broth.

ONLY VEGETARIAN MEALS

| **Prep** | **Portion** | **Cook** | **Per Serving** |
| 10 m | 4 | 10 m | Calories 262; Sat Fat g; Total Fat: 8g; Protein: 26g; Carbohydrates: 38g; Fiber 17.3g; Ca 531mg; K 526mg; Na 690mg |

BRAISED BOK CHOY WITH SHIITAKE MUSHROOMS

1 tbsp coconut oil
8 baby bok choy, cut in half lengthwise
½ cup water
1 tbsp coconut aminos
1 cup shiitake mushrooms, thinly sliced and stalked
1 tsp sea Salt
Freshly ground black pepper, to taste
1 shallot, thinly sliced
1 tbsp toasted sesame seeds

Directions:
1.   In a large skillet over high heat, melt the coconut oil. Add the bok choy in a single layer. Add the water, coconut amino acid and mushrooms to the pan
2.   Cover and braise the vegetables for 5-10 minutes, or until the bok choy is tender.
3.   Remove the pan from the heat. Season the vegetables with salt and pepper.
4.   Transfer the bok choy and mushrooms to a serving plate and garnish with the scallions and sesame seeds.

Ingredient Tip: Replace coconut oil with avocado oil.

Prep
5 m

Portion
4

Cook
10 m

Per Serving
Calories 339; Sat Fat 2g; Total Fat: 13g;
Protein: 12g; Carbohydrates: 49g; Fiber
14.3g; Ca 171mg; K 982mg; Na 900mg

AVOCADO VEGETARIAN WRAPS

1 tbsp avocado oil
1 zucchini, diced
1 small shallot, diced
15.5 oz. canned pinto beans, drained and rinsed
1 1/2 tsp. ground cumin
1 tsp white pepper
1 tsp kosher salt
1 small cabbage, grated
1 large avocado, diced
4 large corn wraps
1/2 cup fresh cilantro leaves, chopped

Directions
1.   Heat the oil in a large skillet over medium heat. When the oil is hot, sauté the zucchini and scallions for 5 to 7 minutes, or until the vegetables soften. Stir occasionally to keep them from burning. Add the beans, cumin, pepper, and salt for 1-2 minutes, or until the beans are heated.
2.   In a medium-sized bowl, mix the cabbage and diced avocado.
3.   Spread the wraps on a clean surface. Divide the bean mixture among the wraps and top with the cabbage and avocado. Garnish wraps with fresh cilantro leaves before serving.

Prep	**Portion**	**Cook**	**Per Serving**
10 m	6	20 m	Calories 122; Sat Fat 0g; Total Fat: 3g; Protein: 18g; Carbohydrates: 6g; Fiber 1g; Ca 12mg; K 326mg; Na 588mg

BAKED COD WITH MUSHROOMS

1½ pounds (680 g) of cod fillets
½ tsp salt, plus more for seasoning
Freshly ground black pepper, to taste
1 tbsp extra-virgin olive oil
1 leek, white part only, thinly sliced
8 ounces (227 g) of shiitake mushrooms, sliced and stemmed
1 tbsp coconut amino
1 tsp sweet paprika
½ cup vegetable broth

Directions:
1.   Preheat the oven to 375°F (190°C). Season cod with salt and pepper
2.   Set aside.
3.   Combine the olive oil, leek, mushrooms, coconut aminos, paprika, and ½ tsp salt in a shallow dish. Season with pepper and toss gently to coat the oil and spices.
4.   Place the dish in the preheated oven and bake the vegetables for 10 minutes.
5.   Stir in the vegetables and arrange the cod fillets on top in a single layer.
6.   Pour in the vegetable broth. Return the dish to the oven and bake for another 10 to 15 minutes, or until the cod is firm but cooked through.

Prep
10 m

Portion
4

Cook
30 m

Per Serving
Calories 674; Sat Fat 6g; Total Fat: 20g; Protein: 24g; Carbohydrates: 102g; Fiber 15.4g; Ca 371mg; K 800mg; Na 972mg

BEEN ENCHILADAS

2 tbsp extra virgin olive oil
2 medium sweet potatoes, peeled and diced (1-inch cubes)
1 red bell pepper, seeded and diced
1 small shallot, chopped
1 tbsp white pepper
1/2 tsp sea salt
1 tsp onion powder
1 tsp garlic powder
1 tsp ground cumin
2 tbsp. crushed garlic
10 oz. canned red enchilada sauce with no added sugar (divided)
3 tbsp. fresh cilantro leaves, chopped (extra for garnish)
15 oz. canned black turtle beans, drained and rinsed
8 corn wraps

Directions:

1.   Coat a large casserole dish with baking spray and preheat the oven to 350°F, with the rack in the center of the oven.
2.   Heat olive oil in a large skillet over medium heat. When the oil is hot, add the sweet potatoes and fry them for 10 to 12 minutes, or until they soften and the edges become crisp. Stir-fry the peppers and scallions for 3 minutes before adding the pepper, salt, onion powder, garlic powder, cumin, and crushed garlic. Let the flavors blend for 1 minute before adding 3 tbsp of enchilada sauce, 3 tbsp of cilantro leaves, and the black turtle beans. Stir until all ingredients are heated and transfer the pan to a wooden cutting board.
3.   Heat the wraps in the microwave for 15-20 seconds. Place the heated, open wraps on a clean surface and pour about 3-5 tbsp of enchilada sauce over each one, spreading the sauce in an even layer. Divide the sweet potatoes and beans among the wraps. Fold the wraps as burritos and arrange them in the prepared casserole dish, with the folds facing down. Pour the remaining enchilada sauce over all the wrappers.
4.   Bake the casserole in the oven for 15 minutes, or until the sauce is heated through and has reached boiling point.
5.   Serve the enchiladas, garnishing them with more cilantro leaves and your favorite toppings.

Recipe tip: Garnishes with Creamy jalapeño ranch dressing, chopped avocado, chopped tomatoes, chopped jalapenos.

Prep
10 m

Portion
4

Cook
10 m

Per Serving
Calories 105; Sat Fat 1g; Total Fat:10g;
Protein: 2g; Carbohydrates: 3g; Fiber 1.8g;
Ca 52mg; K 107mg; Na 183mg

BROCCOLI AND SESAME (STIR-FRIED)

. . . .

2 tbsp extra virgin olive oil
1 tsp sesame oil
4 cups broccoli florets
1 tbsp grated fresh ginger
¼ tsp. sea salt
2 cloves of garlic, minced
2 tbsp toasted sesame seeds

Directions:

1.   Heat the olive oil and sesame oil in a large nonstick skillet over medium-high heat until shimmering.
2.   Add the broccoli, ginger, and salt. Cook for 5 to 7 minutes, stirring until the broccoli brown.
3.   Add the garlic. Cook for 30 seconds, stirring constantly.
4.   Remove from heat and add sesame seeds.

Substitution Tip: Replace olive oil with avocado oil.

Prep
10 m

Portion
2

Cook
15 m

Per Serving
Calories 244; Sat Fat 2g;
Total Fat: 17g; Protein: 7g;
Carbohydrates:27 g; Fiber 13g;
Ca 64mg; K 719mg; Na 892mg

ARTICHOKE AND FRESH MINT RISOTTO

. . . .

4 cups vegetable broth
4 tbsp avocado oil (divided)
1 small shallot, diced
4 oz. sweet peas, chopped and halved
14 oz. canned artichoke hearts, drained and cut into quarters
1 ½ cup Arborio rice
¼ tbsp sea salt
½ tsp white pepper
¼ cup fresh mint leaves, chopped
¼ cup fresh chives, chopped
⅓ cup fresh flat-leaf parsley, chopped
½ lemon, squeezed

Directions

1.   Bring the broth to a gentle boil in a large pot over medium heat. When the stock has heated, transfer the pot to a wooden cutting board while preparing the rest of the dish.
2.   In a large skillet over medium heat, heat 2 tbsp of oil. When the oil is hot, sauté the shallots, peas, and artichoke hearts, stirring, until the hearts soften and the shallots turn transparent about 6 to 8 minutes. Scrape the vegetables into a small bowl and keep warm.
3.   In the same skillet, add the rest of the avocado oil over medium heat. When the oil is hot, sauté the rice and salt, stirring continuously for 2-3 minutes.

Don't be alarmed if the rice starts to crackle, pop, and pop- it's normal. Add 1 cup of heated broth to the pan and stir-fry for 5-8 minutes, or until all the liquid has been absorbed. Continue adding 1 cup of broth at a time and cook the risotto until all the broth has been used up or the rice has reached the desired level of tenderness. If all the broth has been used up and the rice is still not quite tender, add water and continue cooking, using ⅓ cup of hot water at a time.
4.   Pour the cooked rice into a large serving bowl and stir in the pepper, mint leaves, chives, parsley, and lemon juice.
5.   Serve the hot vegetables on a bed of mint risotto.

Prep 15 m

Portion 4

Cook 20 m

Per Serving
Calories 97; Sat Fat 0g; Total Fat:5g; Protein: 2g; Carbohydrates: 13g; Fiber 1g; Ca 15mg; K 137mg; Na 290mg

SWEET KOREAN LENTILS

1 tbsp avocado oil
1 small white onion, diced
2 cloves of garlic, chopped
2 cups vegetable broth
1 cup dried lentils, selected and rinsed
3 tbsp coconut amino
2 tbsp coconut sugar
1 tbsp rice vinegar
1 tsp sesame oil
½ tsp ground ginger
¼ tsp red pepper flakes

Directions:

1.	Over medium heat, add the avocado oil, onion, and garlic to a saucepan. Sauté for 5 minutes, or until onion is translucent.
2.	Add the broth, lentils, coconut amino acid, coconut sugar, vinegar, sesame oil, ginger, and red pepper flakes 2.
3.	Increase the heat to medium-high and bring to a boil. Reduce the heat to low, cover, and cook for 15 minutes, or until the lentils are cooked.

Ingredient Tip: Add 1 tbsp sesame seeds and 2 scallions (sliced) to garnish.

Prep 10 m

Portion 4

Cook 15 m

Per Serving
Calories 293; Sat Fat 3g; Total Fat: 22g; Protein: 14g; Carbohydrates: 17g; Fiber 6g; Ca 310mg; K 389mg; Na 471mg

TOFU SLOPPY JOES

2 tbsp extra virgin olive oil
1 chopped onion
10 ounces (283 g) tofu, chopped
2 cans of crushed tomatoes (14 ounces / 397 g), 1 drained and 1 undrained
¼ cup apple cider vinegar
1 tbsp chili powder
1 tsp of garlic powder
½ tsp of sea salt
⅛ tsp freshly ground black pepper

Directions:

1.	Heat the olive oil in a large pot over medium-high heat until shimmering.
2.	Add the onion and tofu. Cook for about 5 minutes, occasionally stirring, until the onion is soft.
3.	Add the tomatoes, cider vinegar, chili powder, garlic powder, salt, and pepper. Simmer for 10 minutes to let the flavors blend, stirring occasionally.

Prep	Portion	Cook	Per Serving
1 h (Dough rising time)	6	25 m	Calories 680; Sat Fat 3g; Total Fat: 20g; Protein: 37g; Carbohydrates: 98g; Fiber 13.2g; Ca 517mg; K 815mg; Na 844mg

VEGETARIAN PIZZA

. . . .

Dough:

2 and 4 tbsp quick-rise yeast

3 1/2 tbsp brown sugar

1 1\4 cups warm water

1 1\2 cup tapioca flour

2 1\2 cups unbleached whole-wheat flour

1 tbsp kosher salt

6 tbsp extra virgin olive oil (divided)

Toppings:

2 tbsp avocado oil

2 tbsp crushed garlic

28 oz. of canned marinara sauce

8 oz. of button mushrooms, sliced

1 tbsp dried basil

1 tsp dried oregano

16 oz. mozzarella cheese, shredded

2 cups arugula

Directions:

1. Preheat the oven to 475°F, with the rack in the center of the oven.

2. In a medium-sized glass bowl, whisk together the yeast, sugar, and water. Let the yeast rest for 5 minutes on the counter.

3. Whisk together tapioca flour, whole wheat flour, and salt in a large bowl. Add the yeast mixture and half of the olive oil. Mix ingredients together until dough forms.

4. Turn the dough onto a clean, lightly floured surface and knead for 5 minutes, or until the dough is smooth and elastic.

5. Spread the last 3 tbsp of oil on a large, rimmed baking sheet in an even layer. Place the dough on the baking sheet and cover with a damp kitchen towel. Let the dough rise in a warm place for 1 hour.

6. When the dough has doubled in size, knead it again for 5 minutes and roll it out to fit the baking sheet. With a fork, poke holes all over the dough. Place the dough back on the baking sheet and cover with plastic wrap. Allow the dough to rise again for 1 hour.

7. When the dough has risen a second time, use a basting brush to coat the base with avocado oil. Spread the crushed garlic over the base in an even layer. Place the base in the oven for 5 minutes until the garlic becomes fragrant.

8. After 5 minutes, remove the base from the oven and spread the marinara sauce over the garlic in an even layer.

9. Arrange the mushrooms in the sauce and sprinkle with the basil and oregano. Top the pizza with the cheese and bake for 13 to 16 minutes, or until the cheese has melted and the base is crispy.

10. Cut the pizza into slices and serve warm with the arugula.

Prep	Portion	Cook	Per Serving
10 m	2	30 m	Calories 299; Sat Fat 0g; Total Fat: 1g; Protein: 9g; Carbohydrates: 70g; Fiber 9.2g; Ca 27mg; K 837mg; Na 15mg

VEGETARIAN KEBABS

. . . .

garlic-herb marinated tempeh
8 bamboo kebab skewers
14 oz. brown basmati rice, cooked to serve
8 oz. champignon mushrooms, cleaned
1 red bell pepper, cut into large pieces
1 yellow squash, cut into cubes (1.2-inch cubes)
1 small zucchini, cut into slices (1.2-inch-thick slices)
1 red onion, cut into large pieces

Directions

1.   Follow package instructions to marinate tempeh for at least 20 minutes.
2.   Soak bamboo skewers in hot water for 8-10 minutes to prevent charring.
3.   Prepare rice according to package instructions.
4.   Cover a large baking pan with a border of wax paper and preheat the oven to 425°F, with the rack in the center of the oven.
5.   Divide the marinated tempeh and vegetables among the skewers, threading alternately. You should leave about an inch of skewer visible on each side for easy handling. Save the marinade for later.
6.   Place the skewers on the prepared baking sheet and, using a basting brush, coat the tempeh and vegetables with half of the marinade. Bake for 20 minutes before flipping them over and basting with the remaining marinade. Bake, the other side of the skewers for 15 to 20 minutes, or until the vegetables are fork-tender and the edges are crisp.
7.   Drain the rice.
8.   Divide the rice among 4 bowls and place 2 tempeh skewers on each bowl. Serve hot and enjoy.

Prep	Portion	Cook	Per Serving
15 m	6	6 h	Calories 234; Sat Fat 2g; Total Fat:6g; Protein: 41g; Carbohydrates: 3g; Fiber 0g; Ca 31mg; K 728mg; Na 449mg

PORK LOIN WITH CHILI

. . . .

3 tsp chili powder
2 tsp garlic powder
1 tsp ground cumin
½ tsp sea salt
2 1-pound (454 g) pork tenderloins
1 cup broth of your choice
¼ cup freshly squeezed lime juice

Directions:

1.   Mix the chili powder, garlic powder, cumin, and salt in a small bowl. Rub the pork all over the surface with the spice mixture and place it in the slow cooker. Pour the broth and lime juice around the pork into the pot
2.   Cover the pot and set the temperature to low—Cook for 6 to 7 hours.
3.   Remove the pork from the pot and let it rest for 5 minutes.
4.   Cut the pork against the grain into medallions before serving.

Prep	Portion	Cook	Per Serving
15 m	4	25 m	Calories 268; Sat Fat 2g; Total Fat:12g; Protein:5 g; Carbohydrates: 40g; Fiber 10g; Ca 98mg; K 855mg; Na 205mg

STUFFED BAKED SWEET POTATOES

4 medium sweet potatoes
1 tbsp avocado oil
1 small white onion, thinly sliced
2 garlic cloves, minced
1 14-ounce (397 g) can of black beans, drained and rinsed well
12 cherry tomatoes, chopped
½ tsp chili powder
¼ tsp red pepper flakes
¼ tsp sea salt
1 large avocado, sliced
Juice of 1 lime

Directions:
1. Preheat the oven to 400°F (205°C). Using a fork, poke 5-6 holes in each sweet potato
2. Wrap each sweet potato in aluminum foil, place it on a baking sheet, and bake for 25 minutes or until cooked through.
3. Meanwhile, in a large skillet or saucepan over medium heat, heat the avocado oil. Add the onion and garlic and sauté for 5 minutes.
4. Add the beans, tomatoes, chili powder, red pepper flakes, and salt. Cook for about 7 minutes. Remove from the heat.
5. When the sweet potatoes are cooked, remove them from the oven and carefully remove the foil. Cut each potato lengthwise, almost to the base. Open the potatoes to create space for the filling and pour an equal amount of filling into each one.
6. Top with avocado slices and a drizzle of lime juice.

BEEF, PORK & LAMB

SCAN ME! RECIPES' COLOR IMAGES

Prep
10 m

Portion
2

Cook
30 m

Per Serving
Calories 871; Sat Fat 41g; Total Fat: 54g; Protein: 44g; Carbohydrates: 59g; Fiber 11g; Ca 130mg; K 893mg; Na 317mg

THAI-STYLE BEEF WITH COCONUT MILK

. . . .

2 tbsp coconut oil

1 tsp crushed garlic

1 onion cut into wedges

8 ounces (227 g) round steak, cut into strips

2 cups diced potatoes

1 lime

2 cups diced carrots

1 cup coconut milk

½ cup beef broth

Black pepper to taste

Directions:

1.   Heat the wok over medium heat, then add the oil, garlic, and onion and cook for 1 minute.

2.   Place the beef in the wok and cook for 3 minutes.

3.   Add the potatoes and carrots to the wok and stir-fry for 4 minutes.

4.   Add the coconut milk, beef broth, and black pepper and simmer for 20-25 minutes or until the beef is cooked.

5.   Serve hot with vegetables of your choice and a lime wedge to squeeze!

Substitution Tip: *You can use sweet potatoes.*

Prep
5 m

Portion
4

Cook
20 m

Per Serving
Calories 486; Sat Fat 9g; Total Fat:24g; Protein: 32g; Carbohydrates: 34g; Fiber 1.4g; Ca 41mg; K 498mg; Na 910mg

SHIRATAKI RICE AND PORK BALLS

. . . .

1 lb. ground pork

1 small shallot, grated

1 tsp crushed garlic

1 tsp fresh grated ginger

1 tsp kosher salt

1 tsp white pepper

5 tbsp coconut amino (divided)

2 tbsp fish sauce (divided)

2 tbsp. raw honey

14 oz. cooked shirataki rice for serving

Directions

1.   Line a large rimmed baking sheet with wax paper and preheat the oven to 400°F, with the rack in the center of the oven.

2.   In a large bowl, mix the pork, scallions, garlic, ginger, salt, pepper, 1 tbsp coconut amino, and ½ tbsp fish sauce. Using your hands, form balls about ½ inch thick. Place the balls in the prepared baking dish and bake for 15 to 20 minutes, or until the balls are cooked through, and the outside is lightly toasted.

3.   Meanwhile, in a small saucepan over medium-low heat, whisk together the remaining coconut aminos, fish sauce, and honey. When the sauce reaches a slight simmer, lower the heat and cook while stirring for 10 minutes.

When the pork patties are cooked, toss them in the sauce until they are evenly coated. Serve the pork meatballs and sauce on a bed of cooked shirataki rice.

Substitution Tip: *Replace rice with noodle (chopped).*

Prep
15 m

Portion
6

Cook
7 h

Per Serving
Calories 303; Sat Fat 3g; Total Fat:11g; Protein: 49g; Carbohydrates: 2g; Fiber 0g; Ca 31mg; K 839mg; Na 539mg

LAMB CHOPS WITH ROSEMARY

1 medium onion, sliced
2 tsp garlic powder
2 tsp dried rosemary
1 tsp sea salt
½ tsp dried thyme leaves
Freshly ground black pepper, to taste
8 bone-in lamb chops (about 3 pounds / 1.4 kg)
2 tbsp balsamic vinegar

Directions:
1.	*Line the bottom of the pan with the onion slices.*
2.	*Mix the garlic powder, rosemary, salt, thyme, and pepper in a small bowl. Rub the ribs evenly with the spice mixture and gently place them in the slow cooker.*
3.	*Drizzle with vinegar.*
4.	*Cover the pot and set the temperature to low. Cook for 7 to 8 hours and serve.*

Prep
10 m

Portion
4

Cook
30 m

Per Serving
Calories 976; Sat Fat 10g; Total Fat:34g; Protein: 88g; Carbohydrates: 91g; Fiber 14.5 g; Ca 63mg; K 659mg; Na 392mg

BEEF AND GARLIC MUSHROOMS

Beef:
1 kg. boneless beef tenderloin, room temperature
1 tbsp extra virgin olive oil
2 tbsp kosher salt
2 tbsp. white pepper
1⁄2 tsp. chopped dried thyme
1⁄2 tsp garlic powder
Mushrooms:
1 lb. champignon mushrooms, cleaned
2 tbsp. extra-virgin olive oil
3⁄4 tsp. kosher salt
1 tsp white pepper
1 tbsp garlic powder
1 tsp dried thyme

Directions

1.   Preheat the oven to 425°F, with the rack in the center of the oven.
2.   Place beef tenderloin on a wooden cutting board and drizzle with oil. Season with salt, pepper, thyme, and garlic powder, rubbing the spices over the meat. Heat a large, oven-safe skillet over high heat and sear the beef for 2 minutes per side to seal
the juices.
3.   Place the skillet in the oven for 25 minutes for medium cooking. Transfer the skillet to a wooden cutting board and cover it with aluminum foil to keep warm. The meat will continue to cook while you prepare the rest of the dish.
4.   In a large bowl, sauté the mushrooms with the oil, salt, pepper, garlic powder, and thyme until all the mushrooms are evenly coated. Transfer the beef to a serving platter and cover it with aluminum foil to keep warm. Fan out the seasoned mushrooms in the baking dish and bake for 15 minutes until the mushrooms darken and release their juices. Shake the pan at regular intervals to prevent burning.
5.   Slice the beef and serve it along with the cooked mushrooms.

DESSERTS

SCAN ME! RECIPES' COLOR IMAGES

Prep
10 m

Makes
16

Cook
0 m

Per Serving
Calories 449; Sat Fat 18g; Total Fat:35g; Protein: 5g; Carbohydrates: 35g; Fiber 3.8g; Ca 36mg; K 335mg; Na 114mg

PUMPKIN SPICE CHEESECAKE

2 cups raw, unsalted cashews

2 cups toasted pecans

1 1/4 cup pitted dates

1/4 tbsp kosher salt (plus 1/2 tbsp)

1 tbsp filtered water

1 tbsp ground nutmeg

1 tsp ground cloves

1 tsp ground ginger

1 1/2 tbsp ground cinnamon

2 tbsp vanilla essence

1 tbsp molasses

1/4 cup coconut oil, melted and slightly cooled

1/3 cup raw honey

1/3 cup canned pumpkin puree

1/2 cup canned coconut cream

Directions:

1. Cover cashews with a few inches of filtered water in a large bowl. Seal the bowl with plastic wrap and chill overnight or for 8 to 12 hours.

2. Cover a large baking dish with a border of wax paper.

3. In a blender, chop the pecans, dates, and 1 tsp of salt for 1-2 minutes until the ingredients form a sticky dough. If the dough has not yet formed, add the filtered water and blend until it forms. Pour the dough onto the prepared baking sheet in an even layer. Press the dough into the pan with your fingers or a spatula. The bottom of a clean glass will work even better.

4. Drain the cashews in a colander placed over the sink.

5. In a clean blender, blend the drained cashews, remaining salt, nutmeg, cloves, ginger, cinnamon, vanilla, molasses, coconut oil, honey, pumpkin puree, and coconut cream until a smooth batter with no visible nut chunks are obtained. It should take 1-2 minutes in a high-power blender.

6. Scrape the mixture onto the date crust on the baking sheet and use an offset spatula to smooth the surface. Gently tap the sheet on the counter to release any trapped air. Place the sheet on a flat surface in the freezer for 2 hours or until the cheesecake has completely solidified.

7. Cut the cake into 16 blocks and serve.

Prep
10 m

Portion
8

Cook
50 m

Per Serving
*Calories 219; Sat Fat 12g; Total Fat: 15g;
Protein: 2g; Carbohydrates: 21g; Fiber 0g;
Ca 9mg; K 93mg; Na 14mg9mg; K 93mg;
Na 14mg*

GINGER PUDDING

. . . .

½ cup coconut oil, room temperature, plus some to grease the pan
½ cup raw honey
1 banana
1 free-range egg
2 tsp fresh grated ginger
1 tsp pure vanilla extract
2 cups almond flour
1 tsp baking soda
Pinch of sea salt

Directions
1. Preheat the oven to 180°C.
2. Lightly grease an 8-by-8-inch baking pan with coconut oil and set aside.
3. In a large bowl, beat the coconut oil, honey, banana, egg, ginger, and vanilla with a hand mixer until well blended, scraping down the sides of the bowl at least once.
4. Add the almond flour, baking soda, and sea salt. Pour the mixture into the prepared baking pan.
5. Bake for about 50 minutes, or until the cake is cooked and lightly browned. Serve warm.

Prep
10 m

Portion
2

Cook
0 m

Per Serving
Calories 40; Sat Fat 0g; Total Fat:2g;
Protein: 1g; Carbohydrates: 4g; Fiber
0g; Ca 6mg; K 11mg; Na 8mg

CRANBERRY AND WALNUT SLICES

. . . .

1 tbsp dried dates, diced
1 tbsp dried cranberries
1 tbsp flaked coconut
1 tbsp ground walnuts

Directions:

1.   *Mix all ingredients in a bowl.*
2.   *Using your hands, form into a ball.*
3.   *Roll out the foil, then flatten and roll the dough with the palms of your hands to give it the shape of a cylinder.*
4.   *Roll and wrap in foil, then leave in the refrigerator for 30 minutes until hardened before slicing into disk shapes.*
5.   *Serve with fresh fruit.*

Substitution Tip: *Replace walnuts with pecans.*

Prep
5 m

Makes
12

Cook
10 m

Per Serving
Calories 101; Sat Fat 3g; Total Fat:4g;
Protein: 2g; Carbohydrates: 14g; Fiber
1g; Ca 31mg; K 120mg; Na 222mg

COCONUT AND HONEY COOKIES

3 tbsp coconut oil, melted
1 tbsp coconut sugar
2 tbsp raw honey
1 tbsp ground cinnamon
¼ tbsp baking powder
1 tbsp coconut flour
2 tbsp of cassava flour
½ cup tiger nut flour
½ cup shredded coconut
1/3 tbsp. kosher salt
1 jelly egg

Directions:

1.   *Cover a large rimmed baking sheet with wax paper and preheat the oven to 375°F, with the rack in the center of the oven.*

2.   *In a large bowl, whisk the coconut oil, coconut sugar, honey, cinnamon, baking powder, coconut flour, cassava flour, tiger nut flour, shredded coconut, and salt. Whisk in the gelatin egg until all ingredients are well incorporated.*

3.   *Form the dough into 12 balls about the same size. Place the balls on the prepared baking sheet and use the bottom of a clean glass to press the balls into the cookies.*

4.   *Place the baking sheet in the oven for 8-10 minutes, or until the cookies are nicely browned.*

5.   *Allow the cookies to cool on the baking sheet for 10 minutes before serving.*

Tip: *add on the top almonds (chopped).*

Prep
15 m

Portion
5

Cook
2 h

Per Serving
:Calories 259; Sat Fat 10g;
Total Fat:18g; Protein:2 g;
Carbohydrates: 27g; Fiber 5.6g;
Ca 26mg; K 241mg; Na 2mg

BAKED APPLES WITH CHAI SPICES

5 apples
½ cup water
½ cup chopped pecans (optional)
¼ cup melted coconut oil
1 tsp ground cinnamon
½ tsp ground ginger
¼ tsp ground cardamom
¼ tsp ground cloves

Directions

1.   Core each apple and peel a thin strip from the top.
2.   Add water to the pot. Gently place each apple vertically along the bottom.
3.   In a small bowl, mix the pecans (if using), coconut oil, cinnamon, ginger, cardamom, and cloves. Pour the mixture over the top of the apples.
4.   Cover the pot and set it on high. Bake for 2 to 3 hours, until the apples soften, and serve.

Prep	**Portion**	**Cook**	**Per Serving**
5 m	1	0 m	Calories 129; Sat Fat 0g; Total Fat:0g; Protein: 1g; Carbohydrates: 33g; Fiber 4.4g; Ca 39mg; K 448mg; Na 2mg

SOFT BANANA AND MAPLE

1 ripe banana, peeled and thinly sliced
1 tsp pure maple syrup
1/3 tsp ground cinnamon

Directions:

1. Line a large baking pan with a border of wax paper.
2. Arrange the banana slices in a single layer on the prepared baking sheet. Freeze the bananas for at least 2 hours.
3. In a high-powered food processor, chop the frozen bananas, maple syrup, and cinnamon until smooth.
4. Pour the mixture into serving bowls. Enjoy immediately.

Prep	**Makes**	**Cook**	**Per Serving**
15 m	16	**4**0 m	Calories 136; Sat Fat 1g; Total Fat:6g; Protein: 4g; Carbohydrates: 21g; Fiber 3.5g; Ca 53mg; K 229mg; Na 33mg

GLUTEN-FREE OAT AND FRUIT BARS

Cooking spray
½ cup maple syrup
½ cup almond butter
2 medium ripe bananas, mashed
⅓ cup dried cranberries
1½ cups old-fashioned oats
½ cup shredded coconut
¼ cup oatmeal
¼ cup ground flaxseed
1 tsp vanilla extract
½ tsp ground cinnamon
¼ tsp ground cloves

Directions:

1. Preheat the oven to 400°F (205°C).
2. Line an 8-by-8-inch square baking pan with baking paper or aluminum foil and coat the pan with cooking spray.
3. Combine the maple syrup, almond butter, and bananas in a medium-sized bowl. Stir until well blended.
4. Add the cranberries, oats, coconut, oatmeal, flaxseed, vanilla, cinnamon, and cloves. Mix well.
5. Pour the mixture into the prepared baking pan; the mixture will be thick and sticky. Use an oiled spatula to distribute the mixture evenly.
6. Place the pan in the preheated oven and bake for 40-45 minutes, or until the top is dry and a toothpick inserted in the center comes out clean. Cool completely before cutting the bars.

Tip: Replace almond butter with sunflower butter.

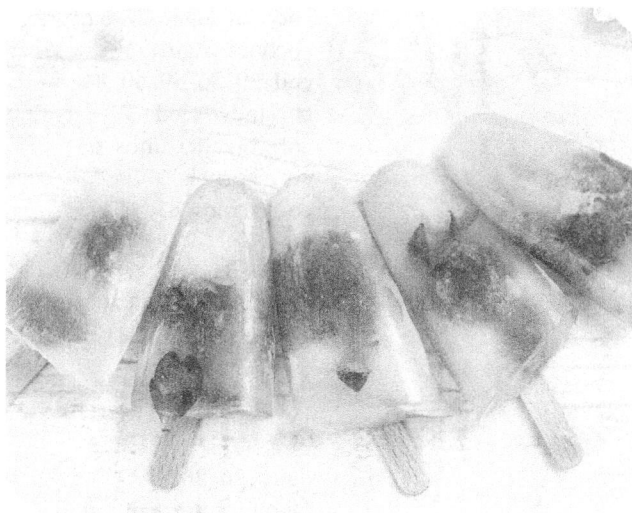

Prep
5 m

Makes
10

Freeze
3 h

Per Serving
Calories 106; Sat Fat 0g;
Total Fat:0g; Protein: 0g;
Carbohydrates: 27g; Fiber 1.5g;
Ca 44mg; K 180mg; Na 5mg

STRAWBERRY MAPLE POPS

. . . .

2 tbsp chopped fresh mint leaves
1 tbsp freshly squeezed lemon juice
⅓ cup pure maple syrup
5 ½ cup chopped strawberries
1 tsp pure vanilla essence

Directions:
1.   *In a food processor, chop mint leaves, lemon juice, maple syrup, strawberries, and vanilla on high speed until all ingredients are well combined, about 1 to 2 minutes.*
2.   *Strain the mixture through a fine-mesh sieve and remove all leaves and seeds. Pour the mixture into popsicle molds and freeze for 3 hours, or until the popsicles are solid. Serve and enjoy.*

Tip: *Replace strawberries with other seasonal fruits.*

Index

Congratulations on making the healthy choice to change your diet. I hope this book has been valuable, provided you with a comprehensive overview of the Anti-inflammatory diet, and gave you the tools to undertake further research. With the Anti-inflammatory diet, you'll find several beneficial effects on your health, including, but not limited to, improving the appearance of your skin, lowering cholesterol levels, helping to prevent the onset of chronic anti-inflammatory based diseases. And all this in addition to losing weight!

Remember not to undergo any significant lifestyle or dietary changes without consulting your doctor, as there may be contraindications.

The first step to making healthier and smarter choices is to make lifestyle changes through a healthy diet, healthy living, and exercise. Follow the 28-day eating plan in this book and eat more natural, unprocessed foods and less packaged, convenient foods to enjoy good health.

APPEAL FROM THE PUBLISHER

Hello, fantastic reader!
I hope you are enjoying this book.

For a small company like us, getting reviews (especially on Amazon) means the possibility to submit our books for advertising. It also means we can just sell a few copies and have a more meaningful effect on society as a whole. So, <u>every review means a lot to us</u>.

We can't THANK YOU enough for this!

Important Notice: We take customer suggestions seriously. If you have any, please write:
<u>info@lizzymcf.com</u> writing in the email object the book's title.

Use the QR code below to download your <u>FREE BONUS.</u>

conversion chart
FOR THE KITCHEN

VOLUME MEASUREMENT CONVERSIONS

Cups	Tablespoons	Teaspoons	Milliliters
		1 tsp	5 ml
1/16 cup	1 tbsp	3 tsp	15 ml
1/8 cup	2 tbsp	6 tsp	30 ml
1/4 cup	4 tbsp	12 tsp	60 ml
1/3 cup	5 1/3 tbsp	16 tsp	80 ml
1/2 cup	8 tbsp	24 tsp	120 ml
2/3 cup	10 2/3 tbsp	32 tsp	160 ml
3/4 cup	12 tbsp	36 tsp	180 ml
1 cup	16 tbsp	48 tsp	240 ml

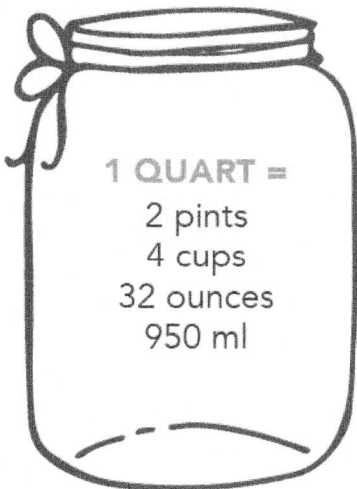

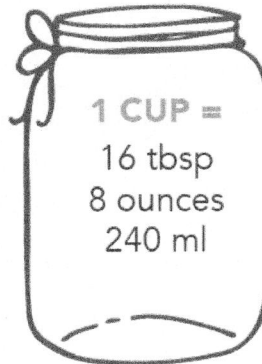

1 QUART =
2 pints
4 cups
32 ounces
950 ml

1 PINT =
2 cups
16 ounces
480 ml

1 CUP =
16 tbsp
8 ounces
240 ml

1/4 CUP =
4 tbsp
12 tsp
2 ounces
60 ml

1 TBSP =
3 tsp
1/2 ounce
15 ml

COOKING TEMPERATURE CONVERSIONS

Celcius/Centigrade	F= (C x 1.8) + 32
Fahrenheit	C= (F-32) x 0.5556

BAKING INGREDIENT CONVERSIONS

BUTTER

Cups	Grams
1/4 cup	57 grams
1/3 cup	76 grams
1/2 cup	113 grams
1 cup	227 grams

PACKED BROWN SUGAR

Cups	Grams	Ounces
1/4 cup	55 grams	1.9 oz
1/3 cup	73 grams	2.58 oz
1/2 cup	110 grams	3.88 oz
1 cup	220 grams	7.75 oz

ALL-PURPOSE FLOUR \ CONFECTIONER'S SUGAR

Cups	Grams	Ounces
1/8 cup	16 grams	.563 oz
1/4 cup	32 grams	1.13 oz
1/3 cup	43 grams	1.5 oz
1/2 cup	64 grams	2.25 oz
2/3 cup	85 grams	3 oz
3/4 cup	96 grams	3.38 oz
1 cup	128 grams	4.5 oz

GRANULATED SUGAR

Cups	Grams	Ounces
2 tbsp	25 grams	.89 oz
1/4 cup	50 grams	1.78 oz
1/3 cup	67 grams	2.37 oz
1/2 cup	100 grams	3.55 oz
2/3 cup	134 grams	4.73 oz
3/4 cup	150 grams	5.3 oz
1 cup	201 grams	7.1 oz

Made in the USA
Monee, IL
27 November 2022